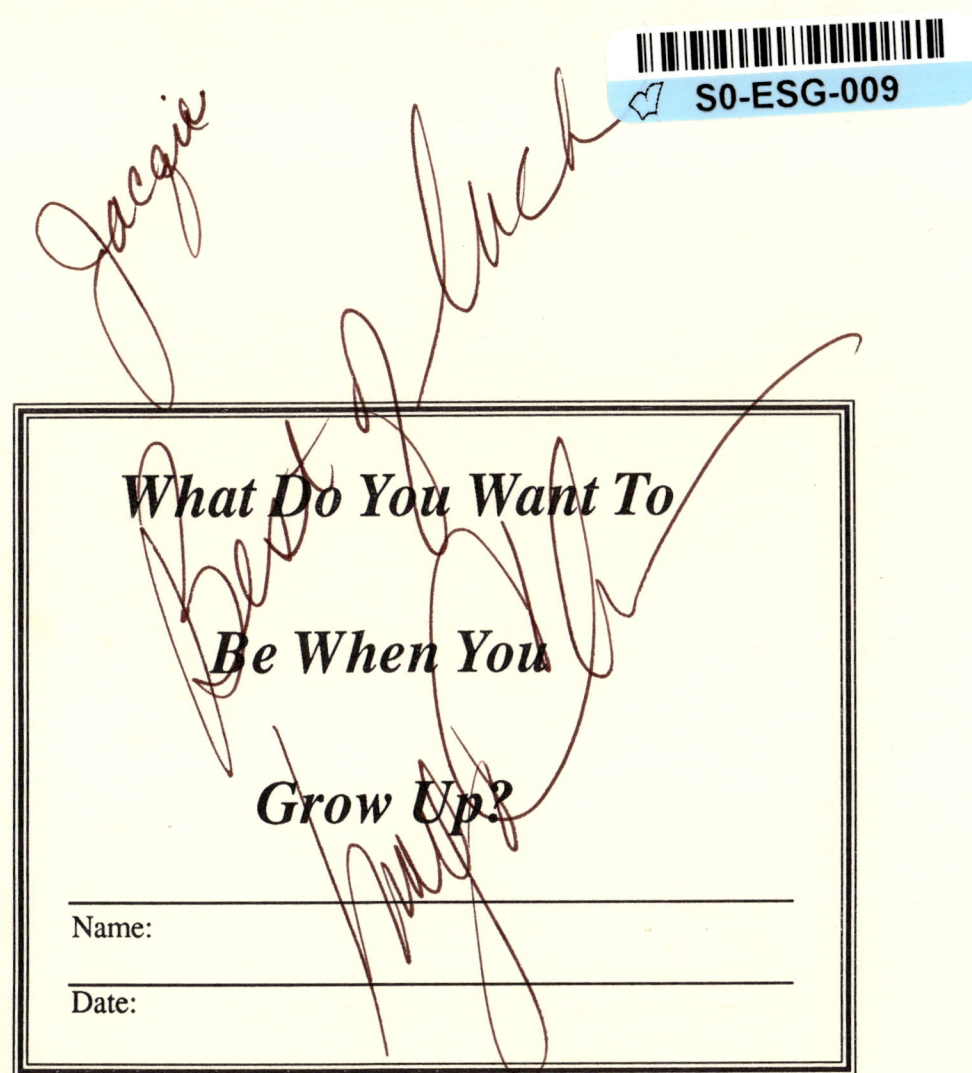

What Do You Want To Be When You Grow Up?

Name: _____

Date: _____

by
Margo Chevers

Grand Publishing Company

Copyright © Margo Chevers 1993
First Printing July 1993
Second Printing September 1993, revised

All rights reserved.
Published in the United States by Grand Publishing Co.

Library of Congress Catalog Card Number: 93-077876
ISBN 0-9636202-0-7

Cover design by Margo Lemieux

Printed in the United States of America

To my children

Michelle and Timothy

who have always been there for me.

They have given me the courage and inspiration

to become more than I ever thought I could be.

Contents

Introduction — 1

Chapter 1
    Background — 6

Chapter 2
    Getting Started — 15

Chapter 3
    Freeing Yourself — 21

Chapter 4
    Wish List — 31

Chapter 5
    Purpose — 35

Chapter 6
    Reality Check — 38

Chapter 7
    My Contribution — 44

Chapter 8
    Power of Belief — 47

Chapter 9
    Tomorrow — 51

Chapter 10
    Putting It All Together — 65

Chapter 11
    Goal Setting, The Key To Success — 75

Chapter 12
    Motivation — 89

Chapter 13
    Obstacles — 93

Chapter 14
    Balance — 98

Chapter 15
    Visualization & Affirmations — 103

What Do You Want To Be When You Grow Up?

Introduction

"I don't know what I want to be when I grow up!"
How many times have you thought this?

It is one of the most frequently spoken statements I hear uttered by adults. But as soon as it has been voiced, most of these people don't do anything about looking for the answers. It is as though they think it would be futile to pursue the thought any further. Or worse yet, that the answer isn't important enough to explore.

Most individuals:

> *... don't take the time or put the effort into designing their lives.*

> *....are satisfied to live a reactionary life. They only take advantage of whatever happens to come along.*

> *....accept whatever happens to them as their life's destiny, whether or not they find it interesting or fulfilling.*

> *....allow themselves to be influenced by*

What Do You Want To Be When You Grow Up?

> *friends or family to accept situations in their life.*
>
> *....don't take personal responsibility for their life's outcome.*

This book has been designed to lead you through a series of exercises that will help you to find answers that are exclusively yours and do it in a way that is as easy as possible.

As a motivational speaker, I have had audience members approach me after a speech and say, "You've inspired me to set goals in my life, and I understand why I need them, but I don't know what I want. After all, *I don't know what I want to be when I grow up.*"

They've been very serious about this. Like most people in society, they tend to go along with opportunities that are presented to them, hoping that these will bring them satisfaction. They go along with these opportunities rather than going through the process of deciding what they want from life or putting together a plan of action.

There are many reasons why people do this. For some it is easier than setting goals and working toward them. Others give in to other people's opinions. The vast majority simply don't know what they want out of life.

These individuals stay in unpleasant or unsatisfying ruts and don't do anything about taking charge of their lives. It seems like too much effort to do something different or too difficult to go through the process of finding out what they want. Therefore, they do nothing.

Most of us have known couples who have gotten married, not because they wanted to, but because they thought they *should.*

What Do You Want To Be When You Grow Up?

They dated for a long time, and everyone around them told them what a perfect couple they were. Pretty soon they found themselves married so as not to disappoint other people.

There are people who, rather than pursue a dream, have grabbed at the first opportunity presented to them only to feel trapped by the situation.

There are others who will enter a profession due to the influence of a guidance counselor, parent or friend, only to find that they don't enjoy that career. They find it easier to continue to pursue that career than to go through the effort of explaining to everyone why they changed their mind. Or very commonly because they don't know what else to do with their lives, they plod along with a vague sense of dissatisfaction.

I have firsthand experience of not living a self-directed life. The first 31 years of my life I lived to satisfy other people and to live up to their expectations. I was tremendously influenced by family and friends. Not only did this keep me from deciding life strategies, *I didn't know what I wanted to do!*

I took a job as a coffee shop waitress simply because my husband knew the owner of the shop was looking for a waitress for the 6AM shift. I didn't want to be a waitress. But the influence of my husband, pushed me into doing something I was scared to death of doing.

You're probably saying to yourself, why did you do that? But think about some of the decisions you've made in your life. Have you ever allowed someone to push you into doing something you didn't feel capable of doing?

In my seminar *"What Do You Want To Be When You Grow Up?"*, I've heard my story repeated by many adults

What Do You Want To Be When You Grow Up?

who have gone into professions unsuitable for them due to the influence of parents and friends. As unhappy as they were, they continued to stay in unsatisfying careers because they didn't want to disappoint other people.

The stories go on and on about individuals who have not made their own choices in life. How they've preferred to go along, rather than make a mistake or rock the boat. They've been inhibited by the thought that making a choice was making a lifelong commitment to something they weren't sure would sustain them for the rest of their life.

One of the reasons I am writing this book is because I was one of those people who did not know how to make personal choices. Nor did I realize that I could actually plan my life. Then I found a process that helped me to make decisions about my life.

I put these ideas to the test, sharing the process with others in a seminar setting. The result has been many participants making life-altering changes.

These changes range from leaving unsatisfying jobs, to writing books, to leaving spouses, to moving across the country, and more. People realized that they can take charge of their own lives and do the things that give them personal satisfaction and fulfillment.

I have written this book as a workbook so that you can use the information immediately. I encourage you to do each of the exercises as they come up in the book. Each one builds on the last one. I have included extra work pages in the back of the book. I encourage you to make copies if you need extras.

What Do You Want To Be When You Grow Up?

Take your time! This is your life, not a test.

> "We cannot become what we need to be by remaining what we are."
>
> Max De Pree, <u>Leadership Is and Art</u>

CHAPTER 1

Background

The process I went through developing what I hope will be an enlightening book includes reading countless books as well as interviewing scores of people who have made life-altering changes. However, I developed most of what you will be experiencing by personally searching for what I wanted in life.

At the age of 31, I sat on the back steps of my beautiful ten room Victorian house. My new car was in the yard, there was a carriage house in the back yard, I had a clothes closet brim full of clothes, money in my pocket, a husband and two children, and I was still asking myself the question "Is this all there is?"

I was miserable with my life but didn't know that I could control it or that I had the power to change it.

To help you understand what brought me to that day, let me take you back in time.

I grew up in the era when women were conditioned to expect that happiness was equated with being married, having children and being taken care of.

What Do You Want To Be When You Grow Up?

In fact, when I was born, I wasn't given a middle name. When I entered the first grade and found out that everyone else in my class had one, I asked my mother why I didn't. The answer was, "When you get married, you'll use your maiden name as your middle name."

Talk about expectations being set up from the beginning! For me it was from the womb!

During my childhood, I lacked confidence in my social skills. I had a difficult time conversing with strangers and the strangest people to me were boys! Obviously, without being able to talk to boys, not many teenage boys had the self confidence to ask me out on a date.

In fact only one ever had the courage to ask me out. But it was a disaster since I was totally silent the entire evening. Not surprisingly, he never asked me out again.

I felt trapped. The expectation was that I would get married and have children. But the reality was that being so shy, I couldn't hold the interest of a boy. Therefore I couldn't see how I would ever be fulfilled as a woman. Consequently, I felt like a failure at the age of eighteen years old.

All around me in high school were other young people who held the same beliefs I did. The girls were graduating with diamond rings for graduation gifts. Some were lucky enough to be getting married within weeks of graduation.

My self esteem, which was low to begin with, plummeted as I saw a future of loneliness and misery for myself. A life of unfulfilled expectations. It never occurred to me to question the validity of those assumptions.

My parents suggested that I get a job. Since that had never

What Do You Want To Be When You Grow Up?

been in my game plan, I didn't know where to start. I teamed up with a girl friend and applied for work at area factories. This was intended as a stopgap while the two of us simply waited for prince charming to gallop into our lives.

One day during our job search, we drove through the small city that bordered my home town. We saw a group of young men hanging out on the corner of the downtown street. Two of them waived and motioned for us to stop. We giggled and sped up, rounding the next corner as quickly as we could. Then we stopped and excitedly discussed how cute they were.

In typical teenage fashion, we repeated our behavior until we convinced ourselves it would be okay to ask for directions. With our trumped up excuse, we stopped. The boys jumped into the car before we even had the chance to say a word. They then suggested that they go with us to show us the way.

I couldn't believe that we were actually picking up boys! That afternoon was exciting as we drove around with these two carefree spirits. Upon questioning, we found out that neither of them had jobs. They spent their days hanging out with a group of other unemployed guys, and they had both just been released from prison.

My tongue loosened up more than it ever had before. I found myself easily conversing with them. Before I knew it, we were making plans to pick them up that evening.

Over the next few weeks, we spent most of our time with our new friends. I kept this a secret from my parents, knowing that they wouldn't approve of the lifestyle these boys led. In fact, I didn't approve of the drinking or their attitude about the law. But it was exciting having someone pay attention to me. Wally in particular, paid attention to me. He talked to me and asked me about myself and even took me home to meet his

What Do You Want To Be When You Grow Up?

parents.

I felt like I really existed. I felt that life could be exciting. Most importantly, I felt that I was important to someone.

One of the factories I had applied at called me and offered me a job on the assembly line. This now gave Wally - who still didn't have a job - and me money with which to have a good time.

I was infatuated by this wild, uninhibited boy. All I could think of was when we would be together next. But my parents had other ideas. They found out about us and demanded that I stop seeing him. They had expected me to go to a Christian college in New York that fall, to meet a nice Christian man, and to marry. They now insisted that I go, thinking that time away would cure me of my attraction to Wally.

Reluctantly I went off to school while Wally (just as reluctantly) went off to jail. He had gotten drunk and stolen a car for a joy ride, was caught, and with his record, was incarcerated.

I wrote to him every week. He only wrote about once a month. But this did not deter me. In fact it only fueled my desire. During my semester breaks, I would visit him in prison. This became exciting and adventurous for me, the shy little girl from the country.

My grades in school weren't good because I wasn't serious about getting an education. When the year was over, I decided that I wouldn't return. Instead, I would go back to the factory where I had worked the year before.

Wally was out of jail by now and we resumed our relationship where we had left off. Since my mother and father still

What Do You Want To Be When You Grow Up?

strongly disapproved of my seeing him and since, in my mind, I was still an obedient daughter, I allowed myself to get pregnant. In my illogical logic, I knew that my parents would want me to get married and give the baby legitimacy.

Somehow in my mind, I still had to have the approval of my parents and since they would expect me to marry the father of my child. In my mixed up logic, this was my way to get their approval about my decision.

Although Wally was drinking heavily, I didn't recognize this as alcoholism. And when he spoke of drugs, I didn't understand that this too was an addiction. But he was hooked on anything that would get him high or anesthetize him from his own personal pain. Unfortunately, this chemical dependency kept him from holding a job or being a responsible husband.

I was the one who had to take on the responsibilities of supporting us. He took on the responsibility of acting like a carefree child. He would go out with his friends all day and half the night, drinking and partying, then when he'd get home, he'd complain about supper not being on the table or dishes sitting in the sink or my not being up waiting for him.

One such night, he added a new twist to his tirade by beating me up. I didn't understand what was happening. I had no idea that men beat up their wives. The feelings of shame and shock from that moment will stay indelibly imprinted in my mind more than the physical pain.

Of course he apologized the very next day. He assured me it had been a mistake and it would never happen again. He was sweet and kind to me. The look on his face expressed such love and caring that I believed him.

What Do You Want To Be When You Grow Up?

Over the next six years, this became a recurring pattern. He would find something to get mad about and take it out on me. He would drag me out of bed to yell at me and demand that I cook for him or clean the house. He would rape me if I denied him his *"marital privileges"*. He would pound me in the face for rebutting something he said. He would even, in a drunken rage, hold a shotgun to my head.

Over the course of these six years, Wally frequently landed in jail. During those times I would go on welfare so that I could stay at home with my two children. I couldn't imagine going out and working to support myself or leave Wally. As crazy as it now sounds to me, I was afraid of being on my own.

All this time, my self esteem sank lower and lower. I didn't feel as though I could change my life or that I could have any control over it. Time and again I would leave Wally and go back to my parents home. But each time, I would return to him, hoping he would keep his promises.

Meanwhile, the welfare department told me of various programs that were available through their office to help me get an education. However, my self confidence was so shattered that I couldn't imagine I was smart enough to get passing grades. I was also afraid to change. I at least knew how to survive in my current situation. But the unknown hid in the shadowy corners of my imagination, ready to destroy me.

So I stayed, trapped!

When my daughter was almost six years old, Wally came home, drunk, and hit me while I held Michelle. It was the first time that I realized that my children could be hurt by this man. This was the turning point for me. I left him to protect my children.

What Do You Want To Be When You Grow Up?

I didn't know what to do. I had no skills, no education, no job, no self-confidence and low self esteem. Welfare seemed, as always, to be the only solution.

I had a part time job as a waitress that helped along with the welfare checks helped us to get by. I was scared and lonely. I didn't know what to do but live from day to day.

My sister looked at my predicament and suggested that I date. You see, she was brought up the same way I was and thought I needed a man to take care of me. I assured her that after my experience, a man was the last thing I wanted.

The truth was, my early conditioning was still strong. I expected a man to take care of me. I wanted to date, but my shyness kept me from having the confidence needed.

My sister, though, was insistent. She told me about a man she knew who was divorced, had his own business, didn't drink (in response to my questioning) and was a nice guy. Finally, I agreed to go out.

We met and fell in love. As soon as my divorce was final, we got married. I tried to put aside the nagging doubts I had about the relationship. I didn't like the fact that he made the decisions without asking my opinion. I didn't like the fact he didn't take me into his confidence about everyday things. And there were many other signs that should have warned me that something wasn't right.

But, I still thought that I needed to be taken care of. That was my upbringing. My mother's face glowed at the thought that her daughter would now be happy in marriage.

Not long after were married, I found a card sent to the house from another woman. I confronted him, but he denied

What Do You Want To Be When You Grow Up?

anything was going on. I preferred to believe him than lose this chance at happiness.

Over the next five years I frequently ignored signs of infidelity. My self esteem, which had been low to begin with, sank even lower.

It was no surprise that the marriage didn't make me happy even though on the outside, it appeared to be ideal.

We bought a ten room Victorian house. I had a new car every two years. I had new clothes in my closet. We vacationed, went out to dinner every week, and I had spending money in my pocket all the time. I focused on all these outward trappings of material consequence, but at a huge personal price.

During this time, his business began to have problems. He neglected paying bills, over-promised to his customers and under-delivered on his services. His personal spending during this time was at a very high level. His creditors and customers alike called me to ask my assistance. I attempted to keep up appearances, but on the inside I was withering.

I had no control of him, more importantly I had no control myself.

After five years of this life, I sat on my back steps, pondering my unhappiness and asking the question: "Is this what it's all about?"

That afternoon's question changed my life. As I sought an answer, I realized for the first time in my life that I was the only one responsible for what had happened in my life.

Up until that moment, I had blamed my misfortunes on my

What Do You Want To Be When You Grow Up?

parents' strict, religious upbringing. On my sister for being prettier, more popular and smarter than me. On Wally for his mistreatment of me. On my second husband for not being the man I wanted him to be. On anything else I could think of that got in the way of my happiness.

But as I sat there, I realized that I had made all the choices that hadn't been good for me. I had to stop blaming Wally, my mother, father, siblings, and everyone else. I had to take charge of my own life.

The only thing I felt I could do was leave my marriage. That decision started the odyssey that brings me to today, and to the writing of this book. I want to share with you how I went from that miserable woman on the back steps to becoming a real estate broker, director of sales and marketing for two convention hotels, property manager, motivational speaker, college instructor, author, dancer, television host, corporate seminar leader and more.

You too can make dramatic changes in your life.

"DARE TO BE"

Margo Chevers

CHAPTER 2

Getting Started

Let's take the first step toward discovering what you want to do with your life. You have all the answers already. You have been storing them up for a lifetime, safely locking them away. It is time to take a peek at who you are and explore your desires.

The exercises you will do are all designed to help you unlock your inner mind. It has recorded all your experiences and feelings, all your triumphs and defeats, all your joys and sorrows, and is ready to reveal its mysteries to you. Your subconscious has been faithfully storing this information so that you can tap into it and draw from the wealth of your own life, to get an insight into what will bring you the greatest happiness.

Too often, in exchange for pleasing others we have learned to ignore what we want. We become so adept at this that we eventually have a difficult time identifying our true desires. This is what often inhibits us from deciding what we want in our lives. Let's free up those inner memories!

On the next page, I want you to draw a map of your life. Choose those incidences in your life that stand out in your memory, or that you feel have significance. For example, few of us remember our birth, yet, I for one would say that that

What Do You Want To Be When You Grow Up?

was the most significant day in my life.

Record any event that stands out in your life. The first day of school, a day spent in a museum, any thing that comes easily to mind.

You may use pictures, symbols, words, anything that represents the incident to you.

I have drawn a portion of my life to give you an idea of what I mean. However, if you have a different idea of how to do it, be as creative as you'd like. After all, this is your life.

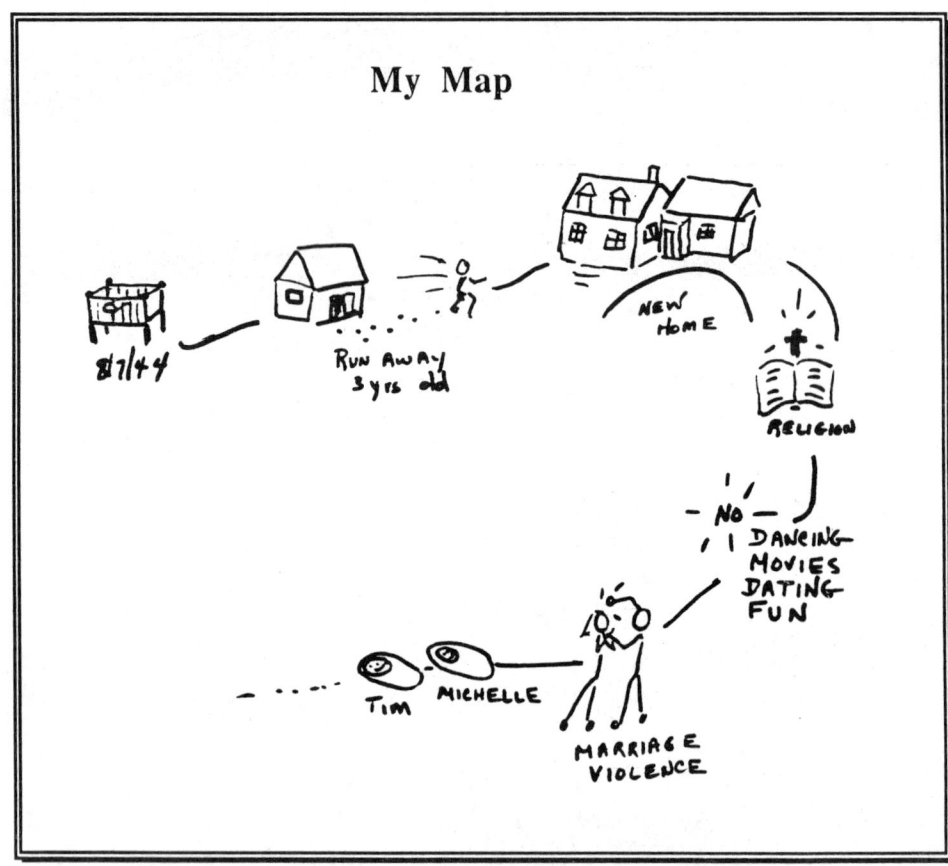

What Do You Want To Be When You Grow Up?

MAP OF MY LIFE

What Do You Want To Be When You Grow Up?

Now that you have drawn a picture of your life, study each symbol, word and picture. Think about why you chose each particular event and what its significance is to you.

Get together with a friend, explain to them what each symbol means, why you chose certain events. Encourage your friend to question you regarding not only why, but how it affected you. If you have no one to do this with, use the space below to write the reasons yourself. (I find this to work best when you use a partner. Many times, we only give surface answers to ourselves. Because other people can be more objective, they can often detect themes or under currents.)

Interpretation of My Map

_____
_____
_____
_____
_____
_____
_____

What Do You Want To Be When You Grow Up?

You can see from my map that one of the events I recorded was an incident when I was only 4 years old. I took off all my clothes and somehow opened the front door. I then proceeded to run away from home.

When I questioned myself about why I had chosen that particular situation, I thought it was only because it had been related so many times throughout my childhood by my mother to anyone who would listen. But when I asked myself what it really meant to me, I realized that it was an act of independence. The removing of clothes and leaving home was a statement of my desire for freedom.

That event, in and of itself, wouldn't have given me great insight into what I should do with my life. But pieced together with the answers to other exercises it helped illuminate what would give me the greatest fulfillment in my life choices.

A participant in one of my seminars was shocked at the number of times education appeared as a theme in her map. When questioned by her partner, she realized that learning was very important to her. However, she had neglected this aspect of her life in recent years. This one exercise helped her identify the vague sense of unfulfillment she had been feeling. She then was able to determine that she needed to do more for herself in this area.

When you have finished this exercise, you should have an understanding of the influences of your previous years. You'll discover those events that were important and why. You'll realize those people who influenced you and how. And you'll understand how you felt and reacted to certain situations, repeated conflicts you've encountered, repeated good or bad behavior, etc. In the space below, write your reaction and what you have learned from this exercise.

What Do You Want To Be When You Grow Up?

MY REACTIONS

_____
_____
_____
_____
_____
_____
_____
_____
_____
_____
_____

"To love what you do and feel that it matters---
how could anything be more fun?"

Katharine Graham

CHAPTER 3

Freeing Yourself

Remember when you were a child how you more readily acknowledged your feelings? You didn't bother to cover up your reactions, but gave into the joy and excitement you felt. As you grew, you learned to accommodate first your parents and teachers, then bosses, spouses and others. In the process, you learned to sublimate your natural responses. There may be times when you want to run outside into the warm summer rain, but the neighbors are just driving up and would think you were crazy. So you tell yourself that it isn't wise to run outside since you'd get all wet and have to change your clothes. Anyway, you might catch a cold and have to stay home from work, losing a day's pay that you need to feed your children. On and on, you can justify not giving in to your impulse with argument after logical argument. You learn to resist the urge and stop yourself before you react to your natural feelings. You do this so often that you don't even recognize your desires any longer.

This is but a mild example of how we condition ourselves. I think, however, you can see how you've been doing this for years. It is a natural reaction to weigh consequences against responsibilities and other people's reactions.

As children, though, we never would have hesitated. We were

What Do You Want To Be When You Grow Up?

more in touch with our feelings, our selfish wants, and better yet, our reasons for wanting things. As adults we've taught ourselves not only to justify denying our desires but also to be so effective at it that we don't think of it as justifying. We believe that we make wise, mature, adult choices.

In a corporate time management seminar I was teaching, I gave an assignment to write down two goals. One business and the other personal. The only criteria for these goals was that they should be accomplished in the one weeks' time between sessions.

One of the women attending the seminar started to sob uncontrollably. She couldn't think of anything to write for a personal goal. She later explained that she was so used to taking care of everyone else both at work and home, that she couldn't allow herself to think of what she personally wanted.

When I gave that particular assignment it was the first time she ever realized that she wasn't doing anything for herself or for her own reasons. Her life was totally devoted to finding out what others wanted, then responding to those needs. *And she believed that they were her own desires.*

I am not suggesting that we shouldn't take care of our responsibilities or that we should stop ourselves from doing something that might not be wise. I am only saying that we frequently cut off our own needs as adults.

Let's wake up our early childhood responses that we have buried for too long. Let's remember some of those exciting, exhilarating moments from our past.

Look back over time and think of something that you have done that gave you a sense of accomplishment. Perhaps you took particular pride in something you did or there was a deep

What Do You Want To Be When You Grow Up?

satisfaction that you felt over some achievement. Maybe you experienced exhilaration or joy or happiness or fulfillment. Whatever it was, write down what you did that made you feel so good. Describe it in detail: exactly what did you do, why did you do it, who else was involved, what time of year was it, what was the result, how old were you, was it school related, church, etc.

I am asking you to relate only one incident. If more than one has comes to mind, relate each of them separately. There is a reason you thought of each of them, and they will become important pieces of this puzzle we are constructing.

My accomplishment

What Do You Want To Be When You Grow Up?

It is now important to look over what you have written and figure out what made you feel so good about this particular incident.

Was it the:

> *challenge of the task?*
>
> *group or person you were involved with?*
>
> *feeling it evoked in you?*
>
> *recognition you received?*
>
> *personal achievement of finishing a task?*
>
> *beauty of what you made?*
>
> *rush of joy you felt?*
>
> *feeling of aliveness you experienced while you were doing it?*
>
> *pleasure of finding a solution through a methodical approach?*
>
> *peace of working alone?*
>
> *creation of something new?*

Let me give you an personal example.

When I was in high school, I entered an art contest which was held each year by the Boston Globe. I won an honorable mention! All the winners were written up in the Globe and I was given recognition at my school.

What Do You Want To Be When You Grow Up?

I was elated that I was the only one from my school that won. Not only had I been written up in the Globe, I was also recognized and praised by my peers, teachers and, in my imagination, tens of thousands of Globe readers. I felt like I was the center of everyone's attention. My ego was stroked as it had never been stroked before.

As a result of this remembrance, I recognized that (1) I liked being the center of attention, (2) I liked to win over my competition, (3) I liked praise, (4) I liked recognition. In my upbringing, these were things you weren't supposed to admit to or pursue. For years I successfully denied that these were important to me. I always felt guilty for feeling good about being competitive or liking praise.

Once I accepted that these were valid feelings because they are MY feelings, I was then able to do things that would satisfy these needs and create a lifestyle that includes them.

It is your turn to go back to the description you wrote about your accomplishments and think about what made you feel so good about your experience.

---

*"Do not wish to be anything
but what you are,
and try to be that perfectly."*

St. Francis De Sales

What Do You Want To Be When You Grow Up?

How I Felt

Besides identifying the positive feelings we need in our lives, we also need to identify those things in our lives that we don't like. We can do that by analyzing those situations that give us the least sense of satisfaction and accomplishment. Too often we continue to work or live with conditions that we literally hate. Yet we tolerate them because we haven't identified the effect they have on us.

I remember a friend in grammar school who lived next to the train tracks. Every time I visited her we were interrupted by the roar of the trains that shook the house. I asked her how she could stand the disturbance. She answered that she was so used to them, she didn't hear them any longer!

What Do You Want To Be When You Grow Up?

The same thing can happen in our lives when we are in a situation that is painful. We anesthetize ourselves to our dislike of what is happening. We fool ourselves by not thinking of our discomfort. Sometimes, we even convince ourselves that we like our arrangement.

I once interviewed a woman on my TV show, "Against All Odds", who had worked for a large bank in Providence, RI. This woman had been born with a jaw that was deformed and was progressively getting more misshapen. Her face was badly disfigured from the sideways growth of her jaw and doctors had told her that there was no hope of ever straightening it out.

She had worked at the bank for a number of years, earning promotion after promotion. She finally became an officer of the bank, high on the corporate ladder.

Her immediate boss at this level was a woman with whom she had a hard time getting along. But she never complained, just continued to work hard. She was pleased that she had accomplished so much as a young woman in the corporate arena.

While working for this boss, she happened to read about a medical procedure a doctor from Boston had recently perfected that could potentially correct her jaw abnormality. She immediately set up an appointment with him. After examining her, he agreed to operate.

Her elation was short lived. Both her boss and the bank's insurance company kept throwing road blocks in the way of her plans for the operation.

Finally, in desperation, she resigned from the job she had worked so long and diligently to acquire, just so she could

What Do You Want To Be When You Grow Up?

have the time and peace she needed to have her operation and recuperate.

It was only after she had quit that she realized how much compromising she had to do simply to get along at work. As she related this to me, she admitted that she had actually hated her job, but had been ignoring the fact.

It's like the background noise of the train that you don't even hear. You don't realize how tense you are from trying to block out the noise until it stops.

Many of you are living under conditions that are depleting your energy. Think of all the roles you play, the responsibilities you carry, and the tasks you perform that give you the least sense of accomplishment. If you could delegate them to someone else, would you do it in a flash? Think of all of these areas of your life, and then write them down on the next form.

Things I Wish Weren't In My Life

What Do You Want To Be When You Grow Up?

Not everything is dismal however. There are things in your life that you wouldn't give up no matter what the incentive. There are things that you are currently doing that invigorate you, make you smile just thinking about them, or give you a warm glow.

Whenever I think about buying a romance novel and reading all day, I automatically begin to relax. I think of the comfort I will experience from escaping reality for a day. I get excited about vicariously living through the heroine's life. And I experience all this before I even choose which book I'll read.

Do you think I would consider eliminating this pleasure from my life? NO WAY!

Likewise, you have things that you feel this way about. Now is the time to list them.

Things In My Life I Would Never Give Up

29

What Do You Want To Be When You Grow Up?

Review these two lists with your partner. Explain to your partner why you continue to tolerate those things from your first list. See if you can explain why you don't eliminate them. Is it because you've stopped hearing the train interrupting your life?

Are you making too many compromises? Do you have a plan to make the changes that you'd like? Is it worth the payoff to keep these things in your life?

Let me explain that there are times when I think we need to make compromises, as long as we know why and for how long.

I compromised before I started my speaking business. I had two teenagers at home who enjoyed eating on a regular basis. I didn't know if I could support them if I was in my own business. So I decided to put off starting it until after my son graduated from school. I have never regretted that decision.

You may find things that you want to change, but it wouldn't be prudent to change them now. You might want to start thinking about ways to modify these areas of your life.

In looking over your second list, think about the frequency with which you do those things you said you'd never give up. Are you doing enough of them? Frequently enough?

What is it about those items that make you feel so adamant about them?

> *"Your only obligation in any lifetime is to be true to yourself."*
> **Richard Bach**

CHAPTER 4

Wish List

This is the opportunity to go back to your childhood. That time of life when you allowed yourself to dream. Remember when someone asked you what you wanted to be when you grew up? You could answer without any embarrassment that you wanted to be a cowboy or a nurse. The next day you could reply that you wanted to be a rock star or an astronaut. And you never felt any conflict from your contradictory answers. You never stopped to think that you weren't being consistent.

Now that you're an adult, you feel that you have to settle for doing only sensible things. You don't dare to dream about having or doing anything that doesn't seem feasible. **You live in a box of familiarity, content to repeat the same things day in and day out.** You even do this with your imagination! No longer do you let yourself fantasize. Your daydreams consist only of the familiar. That's not dreaming.

I want you to imagine that anything is possible for you. That you have the power, the knowledge, the physical attributes, the money, the time, the talent and anything else that is necessary to do what you want. I want you to let your imagination run wild. List everything you've ever wanted to do, to have, to be, to accomplish or anything you've ever wanted.

What Do You Want To Be When You Grow Up?

Without realizing it, you suppress your desires so automatically that you don't even recognize that you're judging your abilities.

For example: If I thought, *"Run in the Boston Marathon"*, I'd immediately dismiss that by rationalizing that I can't even run a mile at the present time. I don't like to get sweaty, it hurts to run, and I'd never have the time to train. I also know that I'd probably quit my training before the first two weeks were up.

I would turn all these rational thoughts into reasons why I had no interest in the Boston Marathon. It would never occur to me that if I actually had the thought of running a marathon, it probably is something I wish I could do. Therefore, it should go on my wish list. Forget the excuses. Just write it down.

Remember, wishing doesn't mean that you have to do it. I simply want you to free up your desires and get in touch with them.

Now it's your turn. Take at least 1/2 hour to free associate ideas. Write down everything. Have fun!

What Do You Want To Be When You Grow Up?

MY WISH LIST

What Do You Want To Be When You Grow Up?

When you are done with your wish list, go back through the items you listed to see if there are any themes. See if there are things that you wrote down more than once. (Sometimes we word things differently, but the meaning is the same).

When I first did this exercise I wrote down that I wanted to live in a castle and be a princess. (Prince Charles was already married so that possibility didn't seem likely.) But I figured out that being a princess meant being special, being treated in a royal manner. The castle symbolized comfort and luxury. When I combined this with the other items on my list, I realized that I needed to create a lifestyle where I felt more important. It also meant adding more material things to my home life.

Go back over your wish list and check off those things that you feel are <u>essential</u> for your life. Mark them with a star (*). Next, go through again and check off those items that are <u>optional</u> (but desirable) with a +. Then go through your list one more time. The rest should only be things which are <u>frivolous</u>. They may be the childhood dreams which lingered into adulthood. Or they may be those things that you've always kept hidden in the recesses of your imagination, but are the frosting, not the cake.

You've just taken a huge step toward deciding which direction you want your life to take.

You should add to this list on a regular basis, going through the same processes you just went through.

CHAPTER 5

Purpose

The question **"Why am I here?"** is one that philosophers and spiritual leaders have been pondering for centuries.

Each of us has a reason for being. That reason is as individual as the person asking the question. It is not a question that is easily answered, nor one that you can dismiss lightly.

This section of the workbook is one that may take you a day, a week, a month or perhaps even years to answer. Once you have embarked on the quest to find out why you exist on this earth, the answer will come to you in time. I personally spent about 1 1/2 years finding the answer. For others, it has only taken days.

To help you search, consider some of these questions.

What one issue, more than any other, creates a passion in you? _____

_____

_____

What Do You Want To Be When You Grow Up?

Do you ever do anything that gives you a deep sense of satisfaction and gratification?

_____

_____

_____

_____

If you only had one day to live, what would be the one wrong in this world you would try to fix?

_____

_____

_____

_____

Look at the answers to these questions. Do they suggest a theme to you? Can you now develop a statement which will describe what you feel your purpose in life is? If you can, write that statement in the box below. If you can't, don't worry. Just think about it for the next few days or months. The answer will come.

I pondered these questions for a long time before I realized that my purpose was two-fold. One was to share information with people to help them understand that they didn't have to hurt. The other was to grow and develop my potential.

What Do You Want To Be When You Grow Up?

My purpose in life is:

"Everybody is talented, original and has something important to say."

Brenda Ueland

CHAPTER 6

Reality Check

How old will you be in 10 years? _____

The answer to this question can be startling. We tend to think of the future as far away. Certainly, ten years from now is too far away for us to be concerned about it right now. But think about it.

Ten years ago, you probably thought today was so far in the future that you didn't give it any thought at all. But in retrospect - from today's viewpoint - it seems that only yesterday you were ten years younger.

What were you doing ten years ago? Were you in school? Married? Having children? How old were they? What were your responsibilities? What things about your life back then did you think would never change? What are some of the things you've done in the past ten years that you never even dreamed of doing a decade ago?

Below, write down where you were financially, emotionally, physically, responsibility-wise, etc. ten years ago.

Were you working? _ _____

What Do You Want To Be When You Grow Up?

How much money were you earning ten years ago?
_____

Where were you working? _____
_____

What was your position? _____
_____

What were your major responsibilities? _____
_____
_____
_____

What was your biggest concern? _____
_____
_____

What was your most prized possession? _____
_____

What did you expect to be doing today? _____
_____

What Do You Want To Be When You Grow Up?

What one thing would you change about the last ten years of your life? _____

_____

_____

_____

What are you proudest of accomplishing in the past 10 years?

_____

_____

_____

What have you done that surprises you most in the past 10 years?

_____

_____

Now, let's look ahead again ten years. It doesn't seem so far away now, does it? Below is a list of questions to answer to help it appear more real.

You will doubtlessly be bothered by two questions as you attempt to answer these questions. "Should I answer as I want the future to be?" or "Should I answer the way I think the future will really be?"

You'll probably use both methods to answer. You'll make judgement calls on each question. Remember, this is your future. No one else has to see this information unless you choose to share it.

What Do You Want To Be When You Grow Up?

I would suggest that if you are in a relationship, it would be very constructive to share your answers with your partner. If your future expectations are diametrically different from one another, you may want to open some communication on this subject. If you can't work out a compromise, then you have some decisions to make.

In ten years my age is. _____

My occupation is (be as specific as possible). _____
_____
_____

My specific responsibilities are _____
_____
_____
_____

My income is _____

My household income is _____

My most prized possessions are _____
_____
_____
_____

My family responsibilities are _____

What Do You Want To Be When You Grow Up?

_____

_____

_____

The most pleasurable experiences I've had these past few years, have been _____

_____

_____

_____

_____

The experiences that have given me the greatest sense of accomplishment in the past few years have been

_____

_____

_____

_____

If you were given an award ten years from today, what would it be for?

_____

_____

At this point, we need to stop and reflect on what we've done

What Do You Want To Be When You Grow Up?

so far. Go back and review your answers to all the questions you have answered so far. Do this before you continue any further. Once you have done that, write down any insights you've had so far.

Do you see any patterns emerging?

Are you surprised at any of your answers?

Have you confirmed some things that you already knew but hadn't taken the time to identify?

Use the following space to record your thoughts.

INSIGHTS

CHAPTER 7

My Contribution

We are all going to die some day. It is a sobering thought but one we all have to face.

Just before I left my second husband, I read the obituary of a woman who was in her early thirties. Just a year older than myself. It stopped me short. I realized that if that had been me, nothing of note would have appeared in my obituary since I hadn't done anything with my life. I decided then and there that I would do things with my life about which I could be proud to have written in my obituary.

In the space below, write your obituary as it would appear if today were the day it was written. List your accomplishments to date.

> " *Our beliefs about ourselves dictate our actions.*
> *Our actions dictate our results.*"
> Margo Chevers

What Do You Want To Be When You Grow Up?

MY OBITUARY

_____
Today's date

_____

_____

_____

_____

Read it over. Is this how you want to be remembered?

As you read your obituary, ask yourself: is this what you would like to have said about you? Most of us wish there were more or different things we'd be remembered for. If this is the case, re-write your obituary as you would like it to read. Write down all those things you would like to be remembered for, the accomplishments you'd like to leave behind, the people's lives you'd like to touch.

What Do You Want To Be When You Grow Up?

MY OBITUARY

_____
_____
_____
_____
_____
_____
_____
_____
_____

"The desire accomplished is sweet to the soul"

Proverbs 13:19

CHAPTER 8

Power Of Belief

Your beliefs about yourself and what you are capable of accomplishing dictate what you are willing to try, or even to dream about. If you believe that you are capable of dancing well, you will get up at a social function and willingly be one of the first people out on the dance floor. But we've all seen an unwilling person refusing to get out on the dance floor with a pleading partner.

The reason one partner wants to dance (besides enjoying it), is they believe they know how. The reason the other person refuses is they don't believe they can dance without making a fool of themselves. As a result, they would prefer to disappoint their partner, than "make a fool" of themselves.

This same principle holds true when we think of doing anything. I happen to hold the belief that I can't add a column of figures in my head. Therefore, I don't even make the attempt. Other people I know hold the belief that they can't speak in front of an audience. So they adamantly refuse. Others won't pick up the phone and ask someone they're attracted to for a date because they believe they'll be rejected. Salespeople imagine they won't be able to close a sale, so they don't ask. Yet, in each of these instances, if the person proceeded to try, I am sure they would survive the experience.

What Do You Want To Be When You Grow Up?

Through practice, they may even become proficient. (To prove this point, I just experimented by adding a column of figures in my head. Guess what? It took a while, but I got it correct!)

When thinking about what you want to do with your life, your beliefs dictate your choices. If you believe that you would make a lousy teacher or spouse or singer or anything else you've ever imagined you'd like to do, but you thought, "No, I couldn't do that," you will find a way to prove your beliefs are correct.

How are your beliefs controlling what you attempt? Think about the areas of your life that your beliefs are influencing.

Are you working below your skill and talent level?

Are you stuck in a job because you believe that no one else would ever hire you?

Do you only stay in a job because you feel that you should, due to the responsibilities you have?

Are you in an unhappy relationship because you are afraid to be alone?

Are you afraid that you are too old, too young, not smart enough, etc., to try something different?

Do you feel like you're sitting on the sidelines of this game called life?

As you answer the next series of questions, ask yourself the above questions in relation to each of them.

What Do You Want To Be When You Grow Up?

WHAT BELIEFS DO YOU HAVE THAT INFLUENCE............

The job you have? _____

_____

_____

The way you do your job? _____

_____

The way you relate to others? _____

_____

_____

Your choice of friends? _____

_____

_____

Where you live? _____

_____

_____

Your self-image? _____

_____

_____

What Do You Want To Be When You Grow Up?

Your present level of success? _ _____

_____

_____

_____

Your expectations of the future? _ _____

_____

_____

_____

> *"Some men dream of worthy accomplishments,*
> *while others stay awake and do them."*
>
> Author unknown

CHAPTER 9

Tomorrow

What is it that keeps some people stuck in a life they aren't satisfied with? Have you ever noticed that there are people who complain about their house, their job, their friends, their car. In fact, there's hardly anything these people seem to like about their lives. Yet, when challenged to make changes, these same people will offer a million and one excuses why they need to continue doing what they're doing.

These excuses are nothing more than self-imposed barriers that protect us from doing something we fear. But we believe that they are real barriers.

Many years ago I heard a motivational speaker explain that **FEAR** is really .

False

Evidence

Appearing

Real

Think about what that statement means. We take evidence

What Do You Want To Be When You Grow Up?

(something we fear will happen) and build it into such a large thought that we convince ourselves that it is real.

To better explain this, let me relate an incident that happened to me a few years ago.

As a single woman with my children grown and living on their own, I was at home alone getting ready for bed. I locked all the doors, turned out the lights, and went upstairs to bed. I immediately fell asleep.

At 2AM, I woke up with a startle. I heard a man outside my bedroom door. He was quietly shuffling his feet toward my room. My heart was pounding so hard that I could feel it banging against the wall of my chest. My mind was in a panic. I tried to think rationally; what could I do?

I first thought of leaping out the second floor window. But realizing the impact could impair me, I tried to think of a better alternative. There was the telephone by my bedside. But I knew that if I called the police, the man would hear a woman's voice and would simply barge through the door. My frantic thinking was slowed to a snail's pace.

Then I reasoned if I just turned on the light, it would show through the bottom of the door. However, the man outside in the hallway wouldn't know how many people were in the room - or even if it was a man or a woman. This appeared to be the best solution. Having made that decision, I willed my arm to raise up and turn on the light, but it was frozen to the bed. I put all my energy into forcing my arm to move, but even as I heard the man outside my bedroom door shuffle closer, I couldn't reach out to turn on the light.

I thought, "This is crazy! Even to save my life, I can't move." And yet, I knew that if I didn't do something, the man who

What Do You Want To Be When You Grow Up?

was now directly outside my door would be in my room in a matter of seconds. But my fear kept me immobile.

I silently screamed out to myself to move my arm. But no, it wouldn't budge.

Then in one lucid moment the whole event came into perspective. I realized that the shuffling noise was caused by a piece of paper that had been blown onto the floor. Slowly it was being pushed down the hallway by the gentle breeze from an open window.

My life had never been in danger! Instead of a 250-pound man outside my door, there was a paper weighing no more than 1/4 of an ounce. My imagination had transformed the paper into a life threatening danger. But to my mind it was a very real danger, and my fear so inhibited me that I couldn't physically do anything that would save my life.

So it is with many of our fears. At the very thought of doing anything new or making any changes in our lives, we often take the smallest piece of information and create an ominous threat. In that way, we can justify why we won't attempt the unknown. The saddest part is we believe our imagination. It becomes our reality. We feel justified in our inertia.

You need to examine your fears. Examine the excuses you are telling yourself about why you are doing what you do and why you aren't doing what you want to. Look at the excuses and recognize them for what they are.

Some of you are saying, "But you just don't understand. I really can't do anything differently."

If you are breathing, you are capable of more than you are currently doing.

What Do You Want To Be When You Grow Up?

On my TV show, I interviewed Fred Meda. Fred is afflicted with multiple sclerosis, and is confined to a wheel chair. However, although he can't walk, he competed in the swimming event in the 1988 Olympics in Seoul, Korea. Granted, he competed in the paralympics. But he didn't say, "I couldn't possibly swim in the Olympics, look at me, I'm in a wheel chair."

Most of us don't have a physical handicap, yet we are more handicapped than Fred because we are unwilling to develop our potential. Instead, we hide behind excuses rather than admit our fears and face them.

Let me share something with you. If you don't get out of your comfort zone (which is to stop hiding behind those excuses), you will always remain where you are! Let me re-phrase that for you. **If you want a better life, then you will have to be willing to do some things differently.**

I shudder to think what I would be doing now if I hadn't stopped using excuses. I would still be on welfare or in an abusive marriage. Or - just as frightening - I could still be in a financially and emotionally bankrupt marriage. While in those relationships, I was actually more afraid of taking charge of my life than I was of being beaten or emotionally abused.

I certainly didn't verbalize it or even admit that to myself. I used all kinds of excuses to stay in those situations because I was afraid. I can still remember some of them.

To justify staying on welfare I used the excuses, *"I can't take care of myself, I have two children who need me at home."* It seems so obvious now, but at the time, I convinced myself that they were better off if I remained on welfare. Yet, the reality was, I eventually got off welfare by going out and getting a job. The result was that my life and my children's lives

What Do You Want To Be When You Grow Up?

dramatically improved.

But, you may be asking yourself, how could you justify staying in an abusive relationship? I had more excuses for that than I had for staying on welfare. My fears led me to believe that my children were better off with an abusive, alcoholic father, than with no father at all. I was convinced that when you got married, you were married for life. The Bible said so. I didn't believe in divorce.

To justify staying in my second marriage, I was terrified of what people would say. *"Look at her, she failed again. Something must be wrong with her."* In my imagination, I thought people would blame me for the bad marriage.

I could go on forever with excuses. The point is, I truly believed all these reasons (excuses) for staying in a dangerous situation.

Now it is your turn to list all the situations you are in, that are not satisfying for you (or are actually not good for you). List anything that creates a negative force in your life.

---

*"I am giddy, expectation whirls me round.
The imaginary relish is so sweet
That it enchants my sense."*

Shakespeare

55

What Do You Want To Be When You Grow Up?

```
┌─────────────────────────────────────────────┐
│      SITUATIONS IN MY LIFE I DON'T LIKE     │
│  _____  │
│  _____  │
│  _____  │
│  _____  │
│  _____  │
│  _____  │
│  _____  │
│  _____  │
└─────────────────────────────────────────────┘
```

Look over your list and answer the question,

"Why do I allow this to be part of my life when it only serves as a negative force?"

As you answer this question, continue to ask yourself "Why?" after each answer. This will help you get to the core of your reason.

What Do You Want To Be When You Grow Up?

```
REASONS I KEEP THESE SITUATIONS
IN MY LIFE
_____
_____
_____
_____
_____
_____
_____
_____
_____
```

As you read over these reasons, do you recognize those that are excuses you use to protect yourself?

We allow situations to continue, either because we are strongly attracted to it or we are more strongly repelled by the alternative. We are drawn to the more powerful emotional force within us. Whichever is the case, we use logical excuses to feel justified in remaining where we are.

To find out the reason behind your excuses, the questions to ask yourself are, "What need does this satisfy in me?" or, "What frightens me so much that I am willing to tolerate this

What Do You Want To Be When You Grow Up?

negative force?" The answers will be found in our emotional motivation.

These answers will probably not come easily. We have spent so many years, in fact a lifetime, learning to protect ourselves. Even to the point of self-deception. Give yourself time to absorb this. Think about it in terms of what your most urgent emotion is.

For example, I like Heavenly Hash ice cream. It is one of my comfort foods. I am easily tempted to eat a bowl of it any time it is offered to me. I can work up such a craving when I think about eating it that I'll go out and buy a gallon late at night. But, if I were told that every gallon of Heavenly Hash ice cream was laced with poison, my strongest desire would be self-preservation. And I would never again touch a dish of it.

I would know the emotional reason I wasn't eating it. I'd be very aware of the circumstances. My desire for the ice cream would still be there, but the desire to live would outweigh my desire for the emotional comfort it gives me.

We make similar choices in our lives about our lifestyles, job positions, friends and lovers.

I have found that a series of self-questions are a valuable technique in our search for answers. Continue to ask yourself these questions until you feel an emotional response in a physical manner.

I have learned to recognize my reaction to my emotions. For example, when I'm nervous, my voice gets shaky. When I'm happy, I feel elation. When I'm sad, tears come to my eyes. When I'm angry, my muscles tighten. When I'm embarrassed, I flush. And on and on.

What Do You Want To Be When You Grow Up?

You are unconsciously reacting to everything in your life. When you are frightened, how does your body react? Does your stomach get queasy? Or perhaps, do your shoulders tighten? Some people feel pressure in their temples, others get a tenseness in some of their muscles. Others get clammy hands or a dry mouth. Many times these reactions are subtle, but they are present when you are afraid.

Think back to the last time you were frightened. How did you physically react?

_____

_____

_____

_____

Now use this concept to discover the excuses you use to keep negative situations in your life. Answer these questions and notice the physical reaction you have. When you feel it physically, you've found a fear. Explore it. Know that it is only a thought that you can work through or put into perspective. With practice, you'll be able to minimize or totally eliminate the fear.

Go back to the list of things in your life that you wish weren't there and use those items to fill in the first blank. Do one of these series of questions for each item to better understand your emotions surrounding them. Then you can do something about it.

What Do You Want To Be When You Grow Up?

If I keep _____in

my life, then I am able to_____

_____

The mere thought of making a change in this area of my life causes me to_____

_____

If I didn't have these excuses to hide behind I'd_____

_____

If I did this, my life would _____

_____

This next exercise is fantasy time. If you had the opportunity to spend one day's time with any three people who have ever lived on this planet, past or present, who would you want to invite?

_____

_____

_____

You probably had a difficult time choosing just three people. But when you made your choices, you did it for some very specific reasons. I want you to list the reasons why you chose each of these people.

What Do You Want To Be When You Grow Up?

_____

_____

_____

_____

_____

_____

Look over those reasons. You probably chose those people because of the attributes they have that you admire. These are things that you would like to have more of in your own life.

For example, one of the people I chose was Margaret Thatcher. I admire her leadership skills. I also like her straightforward manner of communicating, would like to be more influential as she is, would like to have control of events as she appears to have; moreover, I admire her as a woman achieving what is normally considered a male role in society.

I vaguely knew all of this, but choosing Margaret Thatcher confirmed this for me. See if that doesn't happen for you.

These are the things that are important to you. Otherwise, you wouldn't have mentioned them. Are you currently developing these attributes in your life? Do you have the opportunity to use them in what you are doing now? If not, what changes would you have to make to use them?

Are You Having Fun Yet?

I think we all need to have fun in our lives. Remember when

What Do You Want To Be When You Grow Up?

you were a child? It never occurred to you to think about having fun, you just did. But something happens to us as we become adults. We equate adulthood with work and drudgery. We think it is full of responsibility and taking care of other people, making sure the bills are paid, the kids are at their lessons on time, that we call Mom and Dad on Sunday afternoon, and that we go to teacher conference on Tuesday night.

This is what we think being an adult is all about. Rarely do we sit down and say: let's see what I can do to add fun to my life.

Those of us that don't add fun to our lives are the ones that are exhausted all the time. When we don't do pleasurable things, it saps our energy. And we thought we didn't do pleasurable things because we don't have the energy. However, if we did those fun things, we'd be replenishing our energy supply.

Have you ever left work at five o'clock at night, totally spent? You look forward to getting home, kicking off your shoes, turning on the TV and lying on the couch. Your energy level is at a minus 50.

Have you ever had a friend call when you're feeling this way and ask you to do something you normally find enjoyable? But you try to beg off because of your fatigue. Only this time, your friend won't take "no" for an answer. He or she talks you into it. And you find you not only have a good time, but when you get home, you have a tremendous amount of energy.

That's why you need to put fun into your life. You need to enjoy more of what life has to offer.

I want you to list the things you find most enjoyable. Not what you think should be enjoyable, but what you really find pleasure in. It can be a walk in the field, a ride in the country,

What Do You Want To Be When You Grow Up?

curling up with a good mystery, playing with the kids, a rousing set of tennis, or watching an old movie.

+---+
| **THINGS I HAVE FUN DOING** |
| |
| _____ |
| _____ |
| _____ |
| _____ |
| _____ |
| _____ |
| _____ |
| _____ |
| _____ |
| _____ |
| _____ |
+---+

After you have completed your list, go back and place a check mark next to each item you've done this past week. I would venture to say your energy level is quite high if you've checked off two or more of your fun items. If you haven't checked off any, you're probably wondering when you'd ever find the time to do anything that frivolous.

What Do You Want To Be When You Grow Up?

Now, go back and prioritize your items. What do you enjoy the most? Then, set a goal to do one of your priorities. Go through the whole goal setting process that is explained in chapter 11. You'll be amazed at how quickly you'll start feeling better about your life.

You have now completed the foundation for finding the answer to "What do I want to be when I grow up?"

If you have done all the exercises to this point, your awareness about yourself has been heightened tremendously. Also, you have learned your likes and dislikes, the things that excite you and the things you have forgotten were important to you. But you are probably still a little confused as to what it all means.

It is now time to put it all together so you can start making decisions about your life. Stop at this point and re-read what you have written in all the exercises you've completed.

Sanskrit proverb:

"Look to this day
For yesterday is but a dream,
And tomorrow is only a vision,
But today, well lived,
Makes every yesterday a dream of happiness
And every tomorrow a vision of hope,
Look well, therefore, to this day."

CHAPTER 10

Putting It All Together

The next step is critical toward helping you to sort out the information you've gathered. After you answer the following questions, you will allow your subconscious the opportunity to go to work for you.

My recurring themes from the exercises _____

_____

_____

_____

Things that surprised me about myself _____

_____

_____

_____

What Do You Want To Be When You Grow Up?

Things that have occurred to me as I've completed the exercises. _____

_____

_____

_____

The most important things I have found out about myself _____

_____

_____

The things I want to add to my life _ _____

_____

_____

_____

The things I want to eliminate from my life _____

_____

_____

My perfect life needs to include _ _____

_____

What Do You Want To Be When You Grow Up?

The perfect place to live would be _____
_____

The perfect job would include _____
_____
_____

The perfect relationship would _____
_____

My health needs could better be met by _____
_____

I would like to learn to _____
_____

My life needs more _____
_____

My life needs less _____
_____

Your conscious mind has been doing most of the work for you while you've done these exercises. Your subconscious has been listening and storing up information. We now need to tap into the subconscious to help make sense of all you have learned.

I went through many of the exercises I have shared with you

What Do You Want To Be When You Grow Up?

in this book. But it wasn't until my subconscious had enough information that the answers were revealed to me. I spent many years asking myself what I wanted to do with my life.
The answers came to me in a dramatic way which I will try to re-create for you in the next activity. First, let me tell you what happened to me.

In 1984, I had accomplished a tremendous turn around in my life. I had gotten off welfare, become director of sales and marketing for a convention hotel, gone back to school nights, bought a house, and many other things that are symbols of success. But I was still looking for that illusive "thing" that would bring me fulfillment in my life.

One night I turned on television to watch a "made for TV" movie. It was called "The Burning Bed", starring Farrah Fawcett. I knew that the story was about a woman who had been battered by her husband for years and consequently murdered him. I didn't know it would be the catalyst that would change my life.

As I watched the story, I was drawn into the old emotions I had felt when I was married to Wally. I felt the hopelessness, the shame, the humiliation, the victimization, the rejection and a myriad of other emotions. All these emotions left me broken and crying from the self-reproof and isolation of my past experience.

As I felt the emotions wash over me in torrential waves, I simultaneously detached myself from the experience. As I did, I was able to see myself as the accomplished woman I had become. I saw the competence, the intelligence, the emotional stability and all the positive things I had done with my life.

I felt the personal power I had developed over a few short years and revelled in the fact that I never had to experience

What Do You Want To Be When You Grow Up?

hurt like that again. I knew I had learned to take charge of my life and I would never again allow myself to stay in a situation that would cause me that type of pain. I would always be able to call on my inner strength and self love to reject anyone who abused me physically or emotionally again.

When the movie was over, I felt good about myself for all I had done with my life and all that I had learned. Having just experienced the negative feelings that were once the ruling force of my life, and knowing that I now had control of them and the direction of my life, I was giddy with elation.

With my heightened awareness of those feelings, I went to bed. In the depth of sleep, my subconscious took all the information and experiences of my life. Together with the emotion of the movie, my subconscious began to look at the question I had asked years before on my back steps, *"What is it all about? What will I be when I grow up?"*

The experience of the movie was the last bit of information I needed to formulate the answer.

When I woke up in the morning, my subconscious brought the answer vividly to me in the form of a vision. I could sense, feel, and see the answer as it unfolded in front of me. It was revealed that through my experiences, I had learned lessons of life that needed to be shared with others. I would have to do this through public speaking. In this way, I would be sharing answers with others so that they wouldn't have to hurt any longer.

The clarity of the message left no question in my mind that I would become a public speaker. My message would be the steps I had discovered to turn my life around.

The fact that I was petrified of speaking in public and that I

What Do You Want To Be When You Grow Up?

had never shared with anyone the fact I had been abused or a welfare mother, was at that moment incidental. There was no longer any question about what I was to do with my life.

The issue I now struggle with is how to give you, the reader, that experience. I cannot create an emotional catalyst for you. However, you can create that quiet state I experienced in my sleep. And by heightening your awareness through the activities you've done in this book, you, too, should be able to have answers revealed to you.

In order to do this, what I want you to do is find a quiet place and sit or lie in a comfortable position. Put on some quiet music, preferably a New Age recording. Close your eyes and slowly breathe in, deeply. Relax your body and concentrate on your breathing, your heartbeat, and the relaxing feeling of your body. Let your mind go blank. When you have done this for about 3 to 4 minutes, think of a perfect day in the future when you will have everything exactly as you want it. Take yourself through the whole day, from waking up in the morning, dressing in clothes you want, going to the perfect job, being in the perfect relationship. Imagine the perfect setting, the people in your life, the house you live in, the possessions you've acquired. Include everything you need in that day to make it seem real.

When you have finished imagining your day, relax again and slowly drift back into the present. Immediately write down those things in your perfect day that you placed there.

To help you, I am including a dialogue that you can record on tape which will guide you through this activity. Speak in a slow, low tone into a recorder and play it back, following the instructions. Leave long pauses after each new mental suggestion so that you have sufficient time to conjure up images and don't feel rushed.

What Do You Want To Be When You Grow Up?

Dialogue:

"Sit or lie in a comfortable position. Loosen any constricting clothing. Close your eyes and take a deep breath, slowly breathing in.........then slowly breathe out. Notice the cool air you're breathing in and the warmth as you exhale. Again breathe in................ then breathe out. Be aware of your chest expanding and contracting as you breathe. One more time, take your time and breathe in................... and slowly exhale.

Relax your body, start at your feet. Feel the energy leave them as they go limp................ Allow that feeling to flow upward to your ankles....... and calves of your legs........... With the relaxing feeling in your legs, you feel a warmth creeping up your legs.................

Feel your thigh muscles loosen and become heavy with relaxation................. Your hips and lower back are feeling warm and comfortable.......... This feeling is flowing up your back to your shoulders............. Your muscles are releasing all their tension and the feeling is flowing down your arms out to your hands and fingers............ There is a tingling feeling in your fingers as you feel the warmth of relaxation settle in.................

From your shoulders, the feeling is rising up your neck to your cheeks as your jaw relaxes................ your forehead releases any tension it holds............ and the flow of relaxation moves over your skull back to your neck muscles..................

You are now fully relaxed, all the parts of your body feel in perfect harmony with the whole.................... Slowly breathe in again................then exhale..................
Picture yourself at the beach on a warm summer's day.................. There's a balmy soft breeze caressing your

71

What Do You Want To Be When You Grow Up?

skin................ Feel the breeze on your skin and notice how good it feels................... As you look out over the water, you notice the gentle lapping of the waves as they reach the shore............. The rhythm of the sea whispers to you.............. You listen to the murmurs of the waves and feel at peace...................

The sand under your bare feet is warm and inviting............... You lie down on the sand and feel the warmth seep into your body as you become one with your surroundings....................

Listening.......feeling.......enjoying.........relaxing.......allowing yourself to experience the moment.

As you lie there, picture in your mind the most pleasurable lifestyle for you......................

Imagine yourself in your ideal home.......... See yourself in the bedroom of your dream house. It's early morning and you are just waking up to greet the day.......... Slowly explore your surroundings........... Look around the room and notice how large the room is...... the furniture you've chosen......... if anyone is with you........go to your closet and explore your wardrobe.......notice the quality and variety of clothes..........when you are finished looking around your bedroom start exploring the rest of your house noticing the number of rooms........the furnishings.......the wall coverings......any collections you have...........are there other people in the house...........who are they............go outside and look back at your house......notice the style.......the color........the landscaping..........other buildings........

It's now time for you to start your day.... See yourself preparing for the day.........Leaving for work, are you driving? being driven? working at home? travelling?..............Walk into your place of employment and

What Do You Want To Be When You Grow Up?

greet the people you work with.......How do they greet you?......what is your position?.........Do you work in an office?......outdoors?.........with lots of people?........by yourself?...........take your time and explore every facet of your work day..........

It is now the end of the work day. Notice the time and start getting ready for your evening activities. Do you go home?......meet friends?........go to dinner?.........eat with your family?...........Play out the scene in your mind, making sure that it is exactly as you'd like it to be...............................

Now it's later in the evening. Watch yourself in your late evening activities.................................. You've had a full day. You are tired but happy.. Life is good. It is just as you always wanted it to be.........As you slip into bed you reflect back on your day and think of how good you feel about your life. As you drift off you look forward to tomorrow.
You breathe deeply and exhale slowly.....tomorrow will be better than today. Your breathe again and are aware of the cool air filling your lungs............ exhaling you feel your chest contract..........you hear sounds in the room and notice your voice on the tape...........breathe in again and you become aware of the furniture you are on.........exhale and you feel the parts of your body touching the furniture........As you become more aware of your surroundings, you feel the energy returning to your body. You feel good, relaxed and filled with positive expectations. Take your time, when you are ready, open your eyes and stretch."

As soon as you finish this activity, write down those things you saw in your mind that are not now in your life.

What Do You Want To Be When You Grow Up?

<u>**MY PERFECT DAY**</u>

The more often you repeat this exercise, the closer you will come to finding answers for your life. If, on your first attempt, you don't have insights into what you desire, wait a few days. Allow your subconscious to sift through all the information you have given it. Then repeat the exercise, starting with re-reading your responses to all the activities.

As you mentally go through your day, remember: you can revise any of the scenes until they feel as though they are in perfect alignment with what you want in life.

CHAPTER 11

Goal Setting, the Key to Success

If you've been doing all the exercises in this book, you are ready to start making some decisions about what you want in life. It is now time to give power to those decisions.

Goal setting gives you that power. It focuses your energies toward a target. Most people don't achieve success because they haven't first determined what they want to go after. Without that sense of direction, they are easily sidetracked. But when you have a target, you can monitor yourself. You see when what you are doing takes you off course, as well as see the progress you are making.

Living your life without goals is like driving your car out of the driveway without first knowing where you're going. You can cover a lot of road, but you'll also waste a lot of time, fuel, and energy. And you still will not end up where you want to be.

Some of you are saying to yourself that you're not ready to start setting goals. You still don't have any idea what all the information from these exercises means. Don't worry, your subconscious has the answers. You just need to let it sort out the information. The answers will come.

What Do You Want To Be When You Grow Up?

In the mean time, let's learn about setting goals, using this formula.

Personal

First, your goal must be **PERSONAL.** By this I mean that it must be something that you *really* want. It can't be something you say you want because you think it's what is expected of you. And it certainly can't be because you're giving in to pressure from someone else. That is why we have done so much work on who you are and what you've done in the past. Without your personal *want*, you won't work as hard. In fact, you might even sabotage your own success.

I can remember the year I graduated, 1962. The guidance counselor at school advised many of the graduating seniors that if they wanted success (read that, make a lot of money) they should get into the field of computers. After all, computers were going to be the wave of the future.

He was absolutely right about computers being a growing field with many opportunities. But many of the young people took his advice, not because the computer field was their desire, but because someone told them that it was the right thing to do. Many of them found themselves unhappy in a life that someone else had suggested, rather than following their natural inclinations.

Think of some of the young men and women you know that went into a family business because of their parents' expectations. There are many sons and daughters who became lawyers or doctors because it was a family tradition, who looked around in mid-life and wondered why they were unhappy.

What Do You Want To Be When You Grow Up?

When this happens, you'll often see a seemingly successful professional person change careers, family status, and many other things. These changes are a cry to become the individual they always wanted to be. When they finally start doing what they have a personal desire to do, you see a motivated, happy individual.

> *"Cherish your visions and your dreams as they are the children of your soul; the blueprints of your ultimate achievements."*
>
> Napoleon Hill

Positive

The second step in writing goals is to make sure that they are **POSITIVE.** Remember that we are tapping into our subconscious to help guide us toward our target. The subconscious reacts to negative input by protecting us.

For example, you may have tried to diet in the past. But a diet is a negative goal because you view it as giving up the food that you enjoy (a negative thought) and losing weight (another negative thought). As soon as your subconscious realizes that you are going to deny the body of calories, it starts thinking about how to protect the body from starvation. It will create cravings that will sabotage your diet.

I know that when I used to diet, I would start to think about food all the time. In fact, while I was eating lunch, I started planning what I would have for dinner. Or better yet, what

What Do You Want To Be When You Grow Up?

my afternoon snack would be. As a result, I rarely succeeded in staying on a diet, or keeping the weight off.

Another example of a negative goal that vast numbers of people set is to stop smoking. Talk about a negative....the word... STOP! That's saying NO more, NEVER again, GIVE UP. Imagine telling your subconscious these negative words. It reacts by getting nervous at the thought. It tries to think of a life devoid the pleasure of a cigarette after a meal, a cup of coffee, or simply lighting up during a conversation.

I recall a time when I gave a seminar in a woman's prison. I was speaking on the power of goal setting and how it can transform your life and give you back control.

One of the inmates, a pretty young woman, came up to me afterwards to ask how you stayed with your goals once you set them. She said that she had attempted many times to set goals and had gotten excited about them in the beginning, only to fail shortly after starting.

I asked her to tell me her most important goal. She replied that the most important one was to quit using drugs. I suspected that the problem was that she was setting negative goals.

I asked her what she thought of when she set goals to stop using drugs. She said that she wondered how long it would last. She dreaded facing life without the crutch of drugs.

We talked about her goal and how it was negative. She asked how to make it a positive one. I explained that if she set the goal to live a clean and sober life, a life where she had control, she would have a better chance of accomplishing her goal.

I asked her what picture came to mind when she thought of

What Do You Want To Be When You Grow Up?

herself as "clean and sober". You could tell by the look on her face that positive thoughts had come to mind. She said that if she were clean and sober, she could live without the burden of a chemical controlling her. She went on to describe the life she could then have, all of which was positive.

She left, determined to keep the positive picture she had created in her mind, rather than the scary one that quitting drugs had created. If she can maintain that picture in her mind, she will accomplish her goal.

Let's go back to the diet example. Try setting your goal to attain a certain weight. Your subconscious wouldn't have anything to rebel against with that positive goal and would allow you to develop new habits.

For the cigarette analogy, instead of quitting, you could become a non-smoker. That message will create a positive, motivational feeling in you. And you will have an easier time accomplishing your goal.

Specific

Third, your goal must be **SPECIFIC**. It has to be so well defined, that if an eight year old were to read it, they would have a clear picture of what you want to accomplish.

Think of the times when you have said: I want to do better at (whatever you wished to do better than). There is no power in a statement like that. Not only isn't there any power, there is no method of defining when you have accomplished your goal. You didn't get specific enough.

Many people will say, "I want a better paying job." That is so ambiguous that any job that pays more than you are currently

79

What Do You Want To Be When You Grow Up?

making would qualify for success. There are many careers that produce more money than I currently earn, but I'd be unwilling to do them. Drug dealing, bank robbing and the like are some of them.

If it is a better paying job, then you need to identify what you mean by "better paying". Would it be in the same field or even the same company? What are you willing to give in order to get a better paying position? Are you willing to work longer hours? Are you willing to relocate? Will you be willing to go back to school to get extra knowledge? Will this new position fit into your value system, your lifestyle, or your family needs?
Once you have determined all this, you need to write a specific, declarative statement of what you want.

Measurable

Fourth, you need to provide **MEASURABILITY or BENCHMARKS** to let yourself know when you're getting closer to your goal.

If you are on a trip in your car, you know when you are closer to your destination by the number of miles you've travelled, or the name of the city you just passed, or even the amount of time you've been on the road.

This helps you make certain decisions along the way. Like, how much more fuel will I need? Or should I keep going or stop for lunch? Or maybe pull over for the night?

The same is true for your goals. If you have benchmarks you know what needs to be accomplished. If you've set a measurable amount that you can count, you will be able to gauge how far you've gone. You'll also know how much

What Do You Want To Be When You Grow Up?

more you have to do to get where you want to be.

For example, take a simple goal of starting a savings account for your child's college fund. To make this a measurable goal, you need to know what amount will be needed to send your child through college. Then you'll have to figure how many years you'll have to do this in, and divide by that number. This will give you an annual amount. You will probably want to put in a little every payday. How many paydays will you have in a year? Divide the annual amount by the number of paydays.

Let's say that you will need $75,000 to send your child through college. If there are 15 years between now and graduation, that means that you will have to save $5,000 every year toward this fund. You will receive 52 paychecks each year, which means that you will have to put $96.16 into the account each payday.

As you watch the account grow, you will be motivated to keep going. There's something about knowing how far you've progressed, that helps you emotionally to keep going. Also, if you find that tuition has increased or decreased, you'll know how to adjust your savings.

Realistic

The fifth criterion for setting a goal that will keep you on target, is to make it **REALISTIC.** This doesn't mean that it should be something you were going to do anyway. It means that there should be a believability about it. If you don't believe you can accomplish it, then your subconscious will sabotage your success by doing what it believes you can do.

Have you ever had the experience of walking into your boss's

What Do You Want To Be When You Grow Up?

office and asking for a raise that you didn't believe you would get or didn't believe you deserved? You probably were disappointed with the answer, but not surprised.

Did it occur to you at the time that it was your attitude about the results that influenced your boss? The way you asked undoubtedly gave away what you believed. Your body language probably wasn't strong and confident, and your voice was probably weak and less than confident.

You probably didn't pursue the issue when confronted with a negative response because you didn't want to be turned down the second time. After all, you thought the answer would be the same, so why put yourself through the embarrassment of begging only to get the inevitable rejection?

Think of another time when you asked for something. But this time you felt that you deserved to get it. Therefore, it never occurred to you that you might not be successful in getting your wish. This time, if you got a negative answer, you were shocked and asked again, giving a convincing story of why you should get what you were asking for. In fact, you probably were able to convince your boss you were right just by the mere fact that you believed that you deserved it and were willing to try harder to persuade her in your favor.

The same thing happens with your goals. When you are convinced that you deserve to have it, or you believe that it is possible to achieve it, you won't give up. You will continue to persevere because in your mind there will be no reason to give up. But if you don't believe, then you will give up.

Many times, when you don't think your goal is realistic, you will spend inordinate amounts of time preparing. I have seen this over and over again, when friends and acquaintances of mine set out to start their own business. When they have

What Do You Want To Be When You Grow Up?

doubts about the viability of their plans, they spend most of their time doing research, talking to others in business, designing their business cards and letterhead, joining trade associations, etc.

I am not saying that all the above shouldn't be done. However, if you don't believe your goal is realistic, you will find yourself spinning your wheels and talking about your goal. But not doing anything to advance toward it.

If I were to set a goal for myself to run in the Boston Marathon next April, I can guarantee you that I would never be able to do it. Why? Because I don't feel it is realistic. I don't run now, I don't like to run, the furthest I've ever run without dropping in total exhaustion is 1/4 mile. My belief system won't allow me to believe it is possible.

So, you're asking, why would I set the goal to begin with? That would be foolish. Yes, it would. But if I were sitting around with my friends who are runners, and they got to talking about challenges and pushing oneself to the limits, they might throw out the challenge that we all run in the Boston Marathon next year. I just might get caught up in the excitement of the moment and agree to run with them. But the next day, I'd realize that I don't think I can really do it nor do I want to do it, nor would I like to do it. But I can't admit that to my friends and lose face.

You're saying to yourself, "but that's ridiculous." All you have to do is tell them that and they'll let you off the hook. You're absolutely right. But how many times do we allow other people to influence us in setting our goals? Then, we have a conflict inside ourselves between what we have stated we will do and what we believe we can do. I'll tell you right now, what we believe will win out every time.

What Do You Want To Be When You Grow Up?

Deadline

The sixth step is to set a **DEADLINE.** After you have written out your entire goal and determined what you have to do to accomplish it, you need to set a time-line for completion.

This serves two purposes. One is to keep you on track and holds you accountable. When you give yourself a deadline, you will be more apt to do the things that are necessary instead of procrastinating.
This ties right into the second reason. Motivation! Having a deadline is the best motivation I know.

Remember in high school when your English Literature teacher gave you a book report that was due at the end of the semester? When did you read the book? When did you write the report? When I ask this question of the attendees at my seminars, the usual answer is "the night before". When I ask why they waited so long, especially since the teacher had given the assignment months in advance, they all admit it was the deadline that motivated them to get it done. Without the deadline, they never would have gotten around to doing it.

It is the same with our goals. We tend to put off doing things unless we have a time pressure. This book, for instance has been a goal of mine for a couple of years. Whenever I spoke of it, I always had a distant date in mind. But, I decided that the only way to get a fire under me was to set a tough deadline. My deadline was set at December 31,1992.

With this date in mind, I now set aside time on a consistent basis. It is surprising how quickly I was able to get the book done. (The actual completion date was January 4, 1993 only 4 days off my deadline. And I know that if I hadn't set that deadline, I'd still be in the writing process.)

What Do You Want To Be When You Grow Up?

Now that we have the criteria for setting a goal, let's try out a few.

Let's say that you have discovered that as a child you were most alive when you were getting attention. You found out in your 10 year plan that your child-rearing responsibilities will be diminished and you'll have time for yourself in two years. When you went through your exercises at the beginning of the book, you realized that you miss the applause you got in the school play.

I would venture to say that a community theater group might fit into your plans.

Your goal could be "I will be in the Creative Community Theater group production in the fall of 19__"

Is it positive, personal, specific, realistic, measurable and complete with a deadline?

See how easy that was?

Let's take another example. If your answers to the previous questions always involved you with other people and your enjoyment of being with them, you might want to look at adding more people contact in your life.

Perhaps you should have more parties at your home, or join a networking group with people of similar interests.

Let's say that you decide that you want to add people to your life by entertaining more. Your goal could be "I will invite at least four friends over for dinner every other month this year."

Is it positive, personal, specific, realistic, measurable and

85

What Do You Want To Be When You Grow Up?

complete with a deadline?

See how easy it is?

Now that you have an idea of how to do it, let's try your hand at it. Try some sample goals and see if they meet the criteria.

My goal:_____

_____

Now ask yourself, is it personal, positive, realistic, specific, measurable and have a deadline?

Try writing another.

My goal:_____

_____

Again ask yourself if it fits the criteria of a well stated goal. If it does, you are now ready to work on a goal sheet. There are more goal sheets in the back of the book, but for now let's work on the one on the next page.

As we go through the rest of the process, you can fill in the sheet.

"Our greatest glory is not in never falling, but in rising every time we fall."

Confucius

What Do You Want To Be When You Grow Up?

```
┌─────────────────────────────────────────────┐
│              GOAL SHEET                     │
│                                             │
│  Goal _____  │
│  _____  │
│  _____  │
│                                             │
│  Reason for wanting my goal_____  │
│  _____  │
│  _____  │
│  _____  │
│                                             │
│  OBSTACLES        WAYS AROUND OBSTACLES     │
│  _____  │
│  _____  │
│  _____  │
│  _____  │
│  _____  │
│  _____  │
│  _____  │
│  _____  │
└─────────────────────────────────────────────┘
```

What Do You Want To Be When You Grow Up?

ACTION PLAN:

                                                            Start   Finish
                                                            date   date

1 _____

2 _____

3 _____

4 _____

5 _____

6 _____

7 _____

8 _____

9 _____

Attributes I need to develop:

_____

_____

_____

Affirmations to support my goal:

_____

_____

CHAPTER 12

Motivation

Now that you have written down some goals, let's take it a step further.

The big question is why? Why do you want what you've written down?

Unless you have written down a goal that has meaning for you, I can guarantee you'll not accomplish it. You need to have a burning reason for wanting your goal.

By now, I hope that you have found out a lot about your inner passion. Those things that you need in your life that make you feel alive and give your life meaning.

Look at one of your goals and ask yourself why you want that goal. I don't want you to state some purely logical reasons. Now is the time to let your inner self speak and reveal to you why you really want to attain your goal. The more emotional the reason, the more apt you are to maintain your motivation to accomplish it.

Do you recall the first car you bought? Do you remember why you bought it? Most of us don't buy that first car because of the wonderful transportation it will provide. We usually

What Do You Want To Be When You Grow Up?

have a more gut level reason. Something like: freedom to do what we want when we want to. Or friendships, since we know that the kid with the car usually has more friends than anyone else. Some boys even buy their first car so they can get a girlfriend, and so on and so on.

All of these reasons are to satisfy an emotional need and don't necessarily have anything to do with logic. We may justify our decision with logic, such as by telling our parents that it's so we can work and they won't have to taxi us everywhere. But we usually have an emotional reason for wanting it in the first place. (Remember how we talked about this in the chapter about excuses?)

It will take some honest dialogue with yourself to find your *real* reason for wanting your goal.

I used this concept a few years ago when my daughter and I took dancing lessons together and decided to dance a duet in the spring recital.

We chose our costumes and tried them on one month before the event. They were unitards, made of latex that stretched over the body to form a second skin. My daughter who was twenty-one at the time, looked gorgeous in hers. But as I viewed myself in the 360 degree mirrors around the studio, I realized the extra 10 pounds I had put on during the winter didn't look very good on me. Right there and then, I determined that I would lose that weight before the recital, just four weeks away.

I set my goal. Personal? Yes. Positive? Yes, I set the goal to attain my ideal weight (which happened to be ten pounds less than I weighed at the time). Specific? Yes. Realistic? Yes. Deadline? Yes, again.

What Do You Want To Be When You Grow Up?

I then wrote down why I wanted to lose the weight. I listed that I would be more limber, feel better, look better, dance better. The list went on in this vein until I felt I had enough reasons to keep me motivated during the next four weeks.

One week later when I stepped onto the scales I hadn't lost a single ounce. Rather than give up, I went back to re-read the *reasons* portion of my goal sheet. It was then that I realized that all the reasons I'd written down were logical, not emotional.

I then started to ask myself why I felt I needed to lose the weight. My answers were that I was going to dance next to my daughter who was 21 years old and had a firm body. There would be 500 people in the audience, all looking at the two of us. They would be comparing us. Then came the shocker. I was afraid that if I danced this fast dance, without losing any weight, I'd *JIGGLE*.

The sickening feeling I experienced in the pit of my stomach, was enough to let me know that I had found my "Hot Button". I knew this was my emotional reason for wanting to lose the weight. If I could hold that feeling, I would be able to lose the weight without dieting, without ever feeling deprived of food, without any temptation to overeat.

Sure enough, the day before the recital, I stepped onto the scale and weighed in at my ideal weight. Not once during that time did I feel I had to put any effort into it. I just wanted to lose lose weight. My subconscious was my ally and gave me the *want* I needed to accomplish my goal.

Now, I'd like you to write down the reason for wanting your goal. Keep writing down reasons until you feel that you've uncovered the emotional "Hot Button " that will release your motivation.

What Do You Want To Be When You Grow Up?

Reason I want to accomplish my goal: _____

_____

_____

_____

_____

_____

> *"The rudder of the ship is the goal mechanism, the engine is the motivation."*
>
> Author Unknown

CHAPTER 13

Obstacles

The next step in writing your goals is to identify all those obstacles which will inevitably crop up along the way. If you don't identify them, they will not automatically disappear just because you've now decided on what you want.

If you want to start your own business, one of the obstacles might be that you don't have the knowledge to get started. You may not know where the best suppliers are, or you might not know how to manage people.

By identifying each of these as obstacles, you are able to do something about them. But ignoring them will only get you into trouble in the long run. You could have morale problems with employees. Or, you could spend too much money on inventory and end up in trouble with your bank.

Think of all the barriers between where you are now and where you want to be. Write them all down. Don't neglect any of them. They could be the ones that will eventually give you trouble.

What Do You Want To Be When You Grow Up?

Obstacles to my achieving my goal.

_____
_____
_____
_____
_____
_____

Overcoming Obstacles

Now look over your list and think of ways to overcome those obstacles.

What typically happens is that once you have identified the obstacles, solutions become obvious. Then you can put together a plan to overcome those obstacles.

When I needed to lose weight for the recital I had two big obstacles. One was ice cream. The other was snacking while watching TV at night. By uncovering them as obstacles, I was able to devise a plan to ward them off.

One, I didn't buy ice cream. Two, I found alternative things to do at night rather than watch TV. It was actually that simple

What Do You Want To Be When You Grow Up?

once I identified the two main obstacles.

Look over your list of obstacles and think of ways to overcome them.

Ways to overcome the obstacles

_____
_____
_____
_____
_____
_____
_____
_____

It is now time to plan how you're going to accomplish your goal. It is important to know what steps need to be taken, and list them. Then it becomes as easy as following the plan.

First, just brainstorm the various things you can do to get to your target. You don't have to be logical or list things in order. Just write them down as fast as you think of them.

What Do You Want To Be When You Grow Up?

```
┌─────────────────────────────────────┐
│         BRAINSTORM IDEAS            │
│  _____   │
│  _____   │
│  _____   │
│  _____   │
│  _____   │
│  _____   │
│  _____   │
│  _____   │
│  _____   │
│  _____   │
│  _____   │
│  _____   │
│  _____   │
└─────────────────────────────────────┘
```

Look back over your list and number the items in the order in which they should be done. Then, list them in that order. Next, after each item, put a start and finish date, based on your best estimate.

What Do You Want To Be When You Grow Up?

Plan of Action

                                                         Start date   **Finish date**

1. _____
2. _____
3. _____
4. _____
5. _____
6. _____
7. _____
8. _____
9. _____
10. _____

"We cannot direct the wind......
But we can adjust the sails."
Author Unkown

CHAPTER 14

Balance

Before we go any further, it is important to talk about the balance in your life. Some people set goals for their career and finances, but neglect to realize that setting goals in other areas of life are also important. Other people do just the opposite. They set goals in many areas but do not coordinate them so that they are congruent with one another. In either case, these people are setting themselves up for an imbalance in their life.

Let's say you've set a goal to get ahead in your career, and you formed your plan of action to include extra hours at work each week. You also find it necessary to take a night course at a local college, research an important project, and work some weekends. In this case, you've committed yourself to spending a considerable portion of your energy on your career. There's nothing wrong with that unless you have also set a goal to develop a better relationship with your spouse and children and that plan of action includes one excursion a week as a family, working with the kids on their homework three nights a week and spending one evening a week exclusively with your spouse. As you can see, you are probably setting yourself up for failure in at least one of these two goals.

If you charge ahead trying to accomplish both of these goals, you are going to find yourself getting very stressed. More than likely, you'll also get the opposite results from what you

What Do You Want To Be When You Grow Up?

wanted. By planning your goals and checking them for balance, you have a better chance at getting the outcome you want.

Most of us have a number of areas of our lives that we feel are important. When we neglect any of these areas, we have a sense of things not being right. If we don't identify why we feel off center, we sense an incompleteness in our lives. Sometimes we identify what is wrong, and have a knee jerk reaction. We overreact by changing things in our lives that don't relate to the problem.

If you plan your life as a balanced whole, you will need to give importance to all areas of your life. It is then you can achieve more because you won't have the imbalance that is created when you neglect important features of your life.

Look at the circle on this page and imagine that it represents your life as a whole. If you were living your life so that you weren't neglecting any one area of it, it would look as smooth and as balanced as this circle.

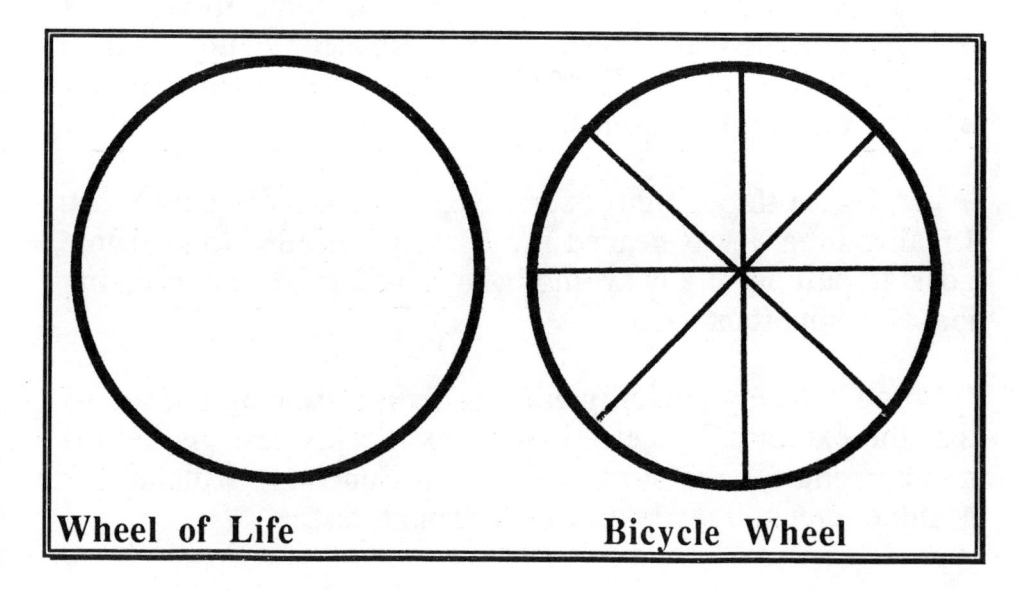

Wheel of Life   Bicycle Wheel

What Do You Want To Be When You Grow Up?

Now imagine that this circle is a bicycle wheel and there are spokes that divide the wheel into equal parts. Each part is an important area of your life. Everyone's life will look different. But most people have in common areas like career, health, family, spouse, financial, social, personal development, leisure, spiritual, community, church, etc.

Measure how well you are doing in each area you designate as important in your life. First, by marking that spot on the spoke of the wheel on a scale from 1 - 10. Then, by connecting each point to create a visual description of how your life looks. That inside wheel you just created is your life as you are living it right now.

At one point in my life, my wheel looked like the wheel on page 102. If I put a wheel like that on my bicycle, how long would I stay upright on my bicycle if I attempted to go on a ride? Probably not long.

Although my career was doing fairly well, my finances were in a mess. I wouldn't have stayed in business very long if I didn't take care of my money. I was under a tremendous amount of stress as a result of my finances being so bad. Another area I was neglecting - because of my efforts in my career - was my friendships.

When I went through this exercise, as I do on a frequent basis, I realized that I was headed for disaster. I needed to set some goals to pull my life back into balance before I lost everything that was important to me.

I started with my health, getting back into dancing classes so that the exercise I received from my weekly lessons helped reduce some of the stress I was experiencing. I planned a healthier diet and made sure I got enough rest.

What Do You Want To Be When You Grow Up?

I then planned to call my friends one time a week, and go out with them once a month.

For my finances, I re-wrote my marketing plan and budget. When I reviewed what I had been doing, I realized I was working hard, but not smart. I found ways to increase my income without increasing the time I was spending.

As my life got into balance, my health and friendships improved. My career became more solid, and financially I became more successful.

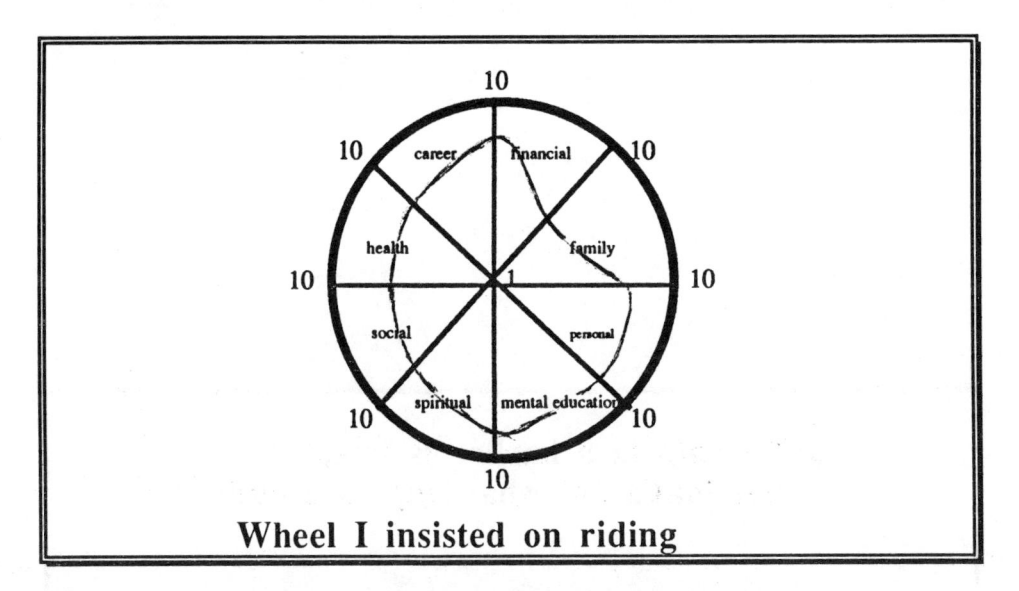

Wheel I insisted on riding

If I had insisted on riding the bike (my life) any great distance in the condition it was in, I'd have found the ride very bumpy. After a while, things would have begun to fall apart and repairs would have been needed. I wouldn't have found the ride too comfortable and would want to get off and quit. I certainly wouldn't have the success I have today unless I had fixed the imbalance in my life.

You are living your life as it is depicted in your wheel right

What Do You Want To Be When You Grow Up?

now. The longer you live your life out of balance the more difficult it will become. The ride will be terribly bumpy. And, unless repairs are made, it will eventually fall apart.

When you are setting goals, take a look at your life as a whole. Then set goals that will bring your life into balance. Compare the commitment you've made to each area of your life to check for compatibility. Check to make sure that you haven't neglected any important area of your life.

**"A ship in a harbor is safe,
but that's not what ships are built for."**

Author Unknown

CHAPTER 15

Visualization & Affirmations

While you are striving to accomplish your goals, you will find that you need to develop certain attributes. Whether it is your ability to interact with people, or to be more assertive about communicating what you want, or to develop persistence, there will be certain strengths on which you will want to improve.

I had to overcome my shyness in order to attain any success during my career growth. It was difficult for me to see myself as a self-confident woman after the life I had lived.

I saw myself as the unsure, unconfident, shy little girl of my childhood. With that mental image, it was difficult to converse with potential homeowners or with meeting planners looking to book hotel space.

In order to live the life I wanted, I knew I needed to develop a new self-image and find a way to believe in myself. I envied other people's ability to communicate with a variety of personality types. I watched other people take on new and exciting jobs and longed to be someone who took chances. But I didn't do anything about it, because I lacked the confidence.

My lack of confidence was a result of the mental picture I held

What Do You Want To Be When You Grow Up?

of myself. It was the mental picture I had acquired through past experience and repeatedly thinking of myself as shy and incapable.

I knew I needed to change the way I saw myself, but didn't know how. Then I learned a method of re-programming my mind through the use of affirmations.

I accidentally discovered how to do this shortly after I started my new life. Being a fan of "Dear Abby", I avidly read her column each day. One of her columns had a list of things to help change a person's outlook on life.

I cut out the column and put it up on my mirror where I would see it every day. I read that column every day for about a month. It had things in it like "I will read one item each day that help my mind grow," "I will speak kindly of others," "I will see only the good in other people," along with other positive input.

I noticed that after a few months, I was acting differently and the results in my life were more positive. And each of the areas in which I acted differently was related to the Dear Abby column.

I was simultaneously reading self-help books. They, also, mentioned affirmations. They recommended changing one's thinking through repetition in a planned and formalized way.

I found that first you must determine those areas in your life you want to change or improve and decide which attributes you need to develop. Then write an affirmation concerning that attribute and repeat it out loud three times a day for one month .

For example, I wanted to improve my ability to talk with

What Do You Want To Be When You Grow Up?

people. My shyness was preventing me from being fluent, causing everyone discomfort. I decided that I needed to be more outgoing and stop thinking of my own discomfort. Therefore, I determined that the attributes I needed to develop were outgoingness and curiosity.

Outgoing people tend to put other people at ease. And curious people, since they ask questions of others, were often quite popular. I figured that if I could be more of these two characteristics, my life would change. Boy, did it.

As I said, I used affirmations. The affirmations I developed went like this:

"I am an outgoing person. I enjoy meeting new people. I am curious about other people and ask them questions to find out about them."

Did you notice the way I phrased the affirmation was as though it was already the truth? I stated it in the present tense. Every statement started with the personal pronoun "I", followed by a number of statements designed to build my belief.

I repeated these statements out loud three times a day for one month. Then, at the end of the month, I put the three by five cards on which I'd written them on my mirror.

I have to be honest with you. Although I have read that you can make major changes in your life in the first month, I've always found that it takes me about 10 months to actually see the changes. But if it works for you in 1 month, that's great. That's all there is to it! Imagine something that simple, having such a profound effect?

Patty, a friend of mine, remarked one day that I was lucky to

What Do You Want To Be When You Grow Up?

be so thin. She dieted constantly and envied the fact that I didn't have to diet. I laughed and told her that I had dieted almost daily for 31 years. I had quit dieting when I discovered that I only needed to change the image of myself in my mind to control my weight.

She was intrigued and asked me to explain what I meant. I told her that I used affirmations to change the way I felt about my body and food.

I shared some of my affirmations with her. *"I am slender. I eat for health. I enjoy being slightly hungry before meals."*

She started using them herself. She was amazed at how her eating habits gradually changed. But one day she was put to the big test.

Patty is an interior decorator. One day, she had taken a client to Boston to look at merchandise in a decorator's warehouse. Around three o'clock in the afternoon, and not having eaten all day, they got on the elevator to leave. In the elevator Patty's stomach was protesting its lack of attention. One of the passengers on the elevator was a young boy. He reached into his pocket, pulled out a chocolate candy bar and unwrapped it in the confines of that small space. The odor of chocolate immediately enveloped Patty. Her stomach groaned with desire.

Wanting to steal the candy bar from the boy, Patty used all her will power to recite her affirmations. Miraculously, her desire for the candy bar left. In its place, she only felt hunger for healthy foods. From that day on, she was a true believer in affirmations.

Another tool for helping build your belief and your self-confidence to accomplish your goals is visualization.

What Do You Want To Be When You Grow Up?

Our subconscious does not know the difference between fact or fiction. When it sees something, it accepts it as the truth and reacts accordingly. Can you remember a movie you have seen where you reacted to the screen as though it were actually happening to you? You either screamed at a scary part, held your breath, tensed your muscles at a tense moment, or had pleasant feelings because of the happiness of the people in the story. Even while these things were going on, your conscious mind knew you were sitting in the movies. However, your subconscious mind reacted as though you were the character in the story.

Using the same concept, you can create your own movies in your mind. But you are the scriptwriter, director, producer and actor. You get to decide what happens on that screen.

In your daily life, when you have done something a number of times, you gain proficiency and confidence in your ability.

By running your own movies in your mind, you create the subconscious reactions of desire, accomplishment, confidence or anything else you want to create.

We did a visualization process earlier. When you made that tape and played it back following the instructions, you were visualizing. The way you used it then was to allow your subconscious to give you answers. You can now use it by seeing yourself accomplishing the goals you have set for yourself.

To visualize all you need is a quiet room and a clear idea of what you want to accomplish. You lie down or sit in a comfortable chair, close your eyes and relax. Breathe deeply three or four times, slowing down your breathing and becoming aware of your body. Slowly think of each part of your body starting with your feet, and feel the relaxation of

What Do You Want To Be When You Grow Up?

each muscle. When you have reached the top of your head and are feeling totally relaxed, think of a pleasant, quiet, restful place you would like to visit. Put yourself into the picture and feel, smell and hear the setting you have created in your mind. When you feel yourself in the scene, then you are ready to begin visualizing yourself successfully accomplishing what you decided on before you began your visualization. Do this in the greatest detail possible.

I would suggest making a tape similar to the last one. Yet this time know in advance what you want to visualize. What are you wearing? What is the physical setting? How many other people are there with you? What is their reaction to you and what you are doing? How are you feeling? What are you saying? Are there smells, sounds, air currents or anything that will help you to experience your scene more vividly?

If there are parts of this you are unhappy with, change it. This is your movie, you are the director and you call the shots. You are the winner! Don't be influenced by "shoulds" and "should nots"".

After you have the perfect scenario worked out and are satisfied with it, stay with it as long as you like. When you are done, go back to that first scene where it was peaceful and quiet. Slowly become aware of your surroundings, then when you are ready, open your eyes and go about your business.

If you repeat this once a day for about 15 minutes each day, you will begin to notice that you will start doing things to make this visualization a reality. Just like with the affirmations this could happen in as little as one month, or take longer. It will depend on how vividly you visualize and how strongly you hold onto your old beliefs.

Remember, you are changing the course of your life by using

What Do You Want To Be When You Grow Up?

these exercises. You may encounter disappointments and obstacles along the way, but stay with it. It is certainly worth it.

Learning and growing are the most exciting and rewarding ventures in life. You will find yourself stretching beyond what you have previously thought possible. But once stretched, you will find that you will not be able to go back.

The entire process I have shared with you in this workbook is one I developed over the course of ten years by reading scores of self-help books, spending hours of quiet time in self-reflection and using the trial and error method. My hope is that you will be able to cut down the time to just a few days or months to find out what you want your life to look like.

You have the rest of your life to perfect it. It is your life and should be lived as you decide it should be lived.

I once heard of a study that was done where the researchers asked elderly people to list those things they regretted in their lives.

Of all the things on the lists, 95% of the regrets were things never attempted. You have the opportunity to start now to reduce your list of regrets.

As you reach your success, please let me know that this book has made a difference.

Good luck!

THE BEGINNING

≈≈≈≈≈≈≈≈≈

What Do You Want To Be When You Grow Up?

Recommended reading

"Psycho Cybernetics"
Dr. Maxwell Maltz

"The Greatest Salesman In The World"
Og Mandino

"Even Eagles Need A Push"
David McNally

"Creative Visualization"
Melita Denning & Osborne Phillips

"Feel The Fear And Do It Anyway"
Susan Jeffers, Ph.D.

"Do What You Love, The Money Will Follow"
Marsha Sinetar

"Think And Grow Rich"
Napoleon Hill

"Absolutely, You Can Create Positive Life Changes"
Charlene Shea

What Do You Want To Be When You Grow Up?

> *"The talent was there all the time, I just didn't see it."*
>
> Margo Chevers

> *"The intensity of your desire governs the power with which the force is directed."*
>
> **John McDonald**

What Do You Want To Be When You Grow Up?

GOAL SHEET

Goal _____

_____
_____

Reason for wanting my goal _____

_____
_____
_____

OBSTACLES　　　**WAYS AROUND OBSTACLES**

_____
_____
_____
_____
_____
_____
_____

What Do You Want To Be When You Grow Up?

ACTION PLAN:

	Start date	Finish date
1		
2		
3		
4		
5		
6		
7		
8		
9		
10		

Attributes I need to develop:

Affirmations to support my goal:

What Do You Want To Be When You Grow Up?

GOAL SHEET

Goal _____

_____

_____

Reason for wanting my goal _____

_____

_____

_____

OBSTACLES   **WAYS AROUND OBSTACLES**

_____

_____

_____

_____

_____

_____

_____

_____

What Do You Want To Be When You Grow Up?

ACTION PLAN:
                                        Start   **Finish**

1_____

2_____

3_____

4_____

5_____

6_____

7_____

8_____

9_____

10_____

Attributes I need to develop:
_____
_____
_____

Affirmations to support my goal:
_____
_____

What Do You Want To Be When You Grow Up?

GOAL SHEET

Goal _____

_____

_____

Reason for wanting my goal _____

_____

_____

_____

OBSTACLES	*WAYS AROUND OBSTACLES*

What Do You Want To Be When You Grow Up?

ACTION PLAN:

                                                                      Start   Finish
                                                                       date   date

1. _____

2. _____

3. _____

4. _____

5. _____

6. _____

7. _____

8. _____

9. _____

10. _____

Attributes I need to develop:

_____

_____

_____

Affirmations to support my goal:

_____

_____

_____

What Do You Want To Be When You Grow Up?

```
GOAL SHEET

Goal _____
_____
_____


Reason for wanting my goal _____
_____
_____
_____


OBSTACLES          WAYS AROUND OBSTACLES
_____
_____
_____
_____
_____
_____
_____
_____
```

What Do You Want To Be When You Grow Up?

ACTION PLAN:

                                                         Start date   **Finish date**

1. _____

2. _____

3. _____

4. _____

5. _____

6. _____

7. _____

8. _____

9. _____

10. _____

Attributes I need to develop:

_____

_____

_____

Affirmations to support my goal:

_____

_____

What Do You Want To Be When You Grow Up?

MY WISH LIST

What Do You Want To Be When You Grow Up?

MAP OF MY LIFE

What Do You Want To Be When You Grow Up?

MY REACTIONS to MAP of MY LIFE

MY ACCOMPLISHMENT
(from page 17)

What Do You Want To Be When You Grow Up?

How I Felt
(from page 19)

What Do You Want To Be When You Grow Up?

Things I Wish Weren't In My Life
(from page 21)

What Do You Want To Be When You Grow Up?

Things In My Life I Would Never Give Up
(from page 22)

Wheel Of Life

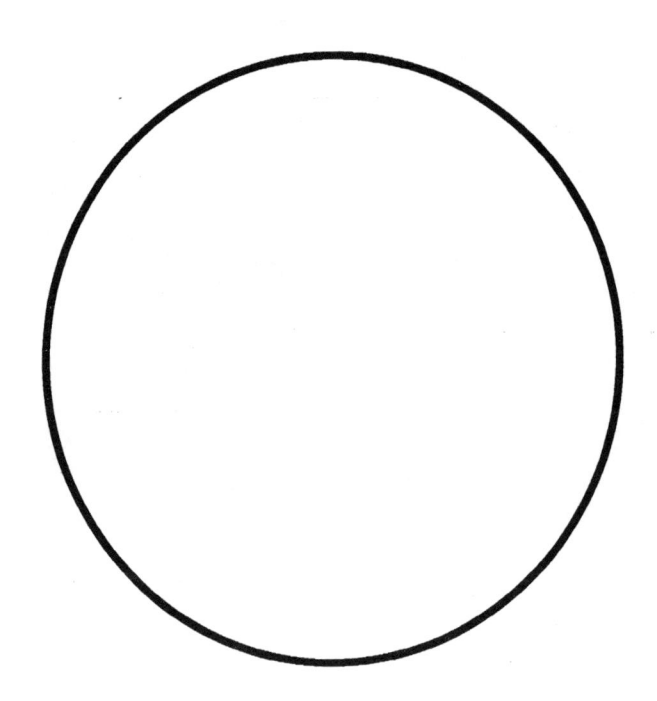

Suggested areas:

Health	**Family**	**Spouse**
Spiritual	**Children**	**Friends**
Community	**Church**	**Education**
Career	**Money**	**Personal**
Hobby	**Leisure**	**Mental development**
Personal growth	**Creativity**	

What Do You Want To Be When You Grow Up?

What Do You Want To Be When You Grow Up?

ABOUT THE AUTHOR

MARGO CHEVERS is an internationally recognized keynote speaker, seminar leader, consultant and author. She is the founder and president of Northeast Leadership Enterprise, Plainville, MA.

Since 1986 she has been delivering messages of substance to organizations and corporations on the skills of Quality Customer Service and Goal Achievement. Some of her clients include Chrysler Corp., The New England Journal of Medicine, New Balance Shoe Co., Department of Defense and many more.

Margo serves on the board of directors of New Hope, an organization which is dedicated to helping families in crisis. A portion of the sales of this book is being donated to New Hope to assist in this work.

Over the past 17 years I have read many books in my journey to recapture control of my life. I have also attended many seminar, consulted with other people and asked advice of many.

Along the way, I have had many personal theories confirmed and have been provoked to re-think some of my old theories.

Much of what has been included in this book is a combination of these readings, seminars, brainstorming and introspections. Along the way, I have re-worked much of what I have learned into what works for me.

There will be vestiges of this vast pool of information in this book. If I have not given credit to the source it is because I no longer remember the source.

I have included a list of recommended readings from those books that made the greatest impact on me. This is not an exhaustive list of all the wonderful books that are available.

To order additional copies of *What Do You What To Be When You Grow Up?*, please indicate your order on the form below. Enclose a check or money order and return to:

Grand Publishing
P.O. Box 1584
Plainville, MA 02762

Inquiries: Call toll free (800) 858-0797 Fax: (508) 643-2978

Please allow 4-6 weeks delivery.

Please send _____copies @ $14.95 each.
Add $2.00 postage and handling.

Name:_____ Phone:_____

Street:_____

City:_____State:_____ Zip:_____

Discounts offered with volume purchase.

20 - 100 copies @ 10%

101 or more copies @ 20%